The Art of Cooking

A Chef's Life Story

Peter C. Brenner

ISBN: 979-8-3303-6531-9

Dedication

I will dedicate my book to my mother, Eleanor M. Brenner, my father, Peter C. Brenner Sr., and my grandmother, Elizabeth P. Brenner.

Acknowledgment

I would like to thank everyone that I have crossed paths with throughout my career. Due to my career spanning four decades, I've met very talented Executive Chefs, Sous Chefs, and Cooks, as well as very hard-working stewarding employees who help make a kitchen run efficiently.

If I mentioned all of you, the list would be very long, but if you are reading this, you know who you are. I would like to thank everyone who has been part of the Colorado Denver Chapter of The American Culinary Federation for their help with my career and their dedication to the Culinary Arts. I would also like to thank the staff at Auguste Escoffier School of Culinary Arts, where I participated and graduated from the Baking and Pastry program. Similarly, I want to thank my friends and family for their support and encouragement with my career, especially my best friend and partner in marriage, Anne K. Brenner.

Working in the food and beverage industry involves working a lot of unusual hours that oftentimes include nights, weekends, and holidays. Anne has supported me through the good and the bad, as well as my success and failure. Much of our happiness has been a direct result of our relationship with both her extended family and mine. Throughout my career, I have had the pleasure of serving guests and employees and have been given praise for my

ability to provide great-tasting, fresh, and nutritious food.
I thank all of you that I have served.

Contents

About the Author

Peter Brenner is an award-winning and versatile cooking professional with over thirty years of experience in four-star hotel culinary programs, corporate chains, country clubs, and private restaurant ownership. He is a self-motivated executive-level chef with current certification as CEC recognized by the American Culinary Federation.

Peter has strong staff management, training, and development skills that allow him to create a cohesive environment. He has worked in various roles such as Chef de Cuisine, Lead Cook, Garde Manager, Banquet Chef, and Assistant Pastry Chef. Peter has achieved first place in two professional cooking competitions at the Pro-Am Celebrity Cooking Classic in Denver, Colorado, and has also won five bronze medals in sanctioned ACF competitions.

In addition to his culinary achievements, Peter has also proven to be a successful business owner and operating partner of a casual upscale restaurant. He values education and attended Nasson College in Springvale, ME, where he studied Liberal Arts and Recreation Programs for two years.

Preface

Welcome to the kitchen of my life, where each chapter is a recipe and every page holds a secret ingredient. As I pen down the journey that led me from a curious kid in my grandmother's kitchen to a seasoned chef, a member of the American Culinary Federation since 2000, and certified as CEC since 2005 with a pantheon of experiences, I invite you to savor the stories that simmer within these pages.

This isn't your typical cookbook, nor is it a conventional memoir. It's a collection of tales sprinkled with the flavors of laughter, the heat of challenges, and the unmistakable aroma of a lifelong love affair with food. Picture a bustling kitchen, the clatter of utensils, and the warmth of shared meals – that's the ambiance I aim to recreate for you.

In the following chapters, you'll find not just recipes but edible bookmarks in the novel of my life. Each dish has a tale – a moment frozen in time when ingredients transformed into memories.

Whether you're a culinary enthusiast, an aspiring chef, or simply someone who enjoys a good story, I invite you to pull up a chair at my virtual table. Let the anecdotes and recipes resonate with the sizzle of excitement and the comforting hum of familiarity. This isn't just a book; it's an invitation to a flavorful journey.

So, as we board on this adventure together, may your curiosity be piqued, your taste buds teased, and your hunger for a good story satisfied.

Bon appétit!

– Peter C. Brenner Jr

Chapter 1
My Beginnings

A stranger would never know what my life has been like from the outside unless he walked in my shoes. Growing up, I've had many experiences in life that have shaped my perspective and led me to follow a path I'm currently content with. In short, I've lived a great life. It has filled me with delight. It brings me great joy to share what has inspired me and continues to make my days better.

In this book, I uncover how I got where I am right now and all the skills I've learned throughout the years. I hope to inspire people in any way that I can.

I was born in 1960 in New Jersey. I belong to a middle-class family. My dad runs a business, and my mother is a homemaker. She is of Italian descent and was usually the one who prepared all our meals for us. Ever since I was a toddler and learned how to crawl, I would enter the kitchen because I was always so curious about things. I would pull open drawers and search through the cabinets. Even as a kid, I loved exploring.

I think it's crazy that the things you grow to be passionate about are ingrained so early. As a child, I was drawn to watching my mom cook, unaware I would make that my career path years from then.

When I was little, I had this tricycle I would take with me to ride around town. I was always eager to explore in my childhood. As soon as I learned how to climb over the fence, I would ride around town for more adventure. When I turned five, we moved to a new town called Cinnaminson. It was pretty around there. I loved watching the sun come out and catching the sunset every evening.

My mother was very good at cooking, and I would always observe her skills. Eventually, one day, I got an opportunity to bake something too. In third grade, my teacher announced a bake sale. All of us had to bake something and bring it in. The judges were going to mark us based on who did best, and the winner would get a reward. It excited me so much. When I got home, I told my mom about it excitedly.

I loved my mom's apple pies, so I convinced her to help me bake them. This was the beginning of my increased interest in cooking.

Another part of growing up was that my family had a summer camp in Maine. We traveled every summer from New Jersey up the coast to the camp in Maine, and we spent time with my grandmother.

Maine has a huge seafood industry. One of the things I loved was we had New England clambake every summer. We went to buy lobsters, clams, and fish. Looking back on it now, those were some of the best days of my life.

My grandfather on my father's side had passed away a month after I was born, and my grandmother, Elizabeth, inherited the camp in Maine. We went to spend the summer holidays with my grandmother on my father's side. She lived in Staten Island, New York.

My grandfather on my mother's side died a couple of months before I was born. My grandmother on my mother's side lived until I was 12 years old. I didn't get to know either of my grandfathers much.

We would go there on holidays and spend time at my grandmother's house. Both sides of my family were very food-oriented and accustomed to good quality food. As I said, my mother's side of the family was Italian, and my dad's side was German, Irish, Scottish, and English. They were much more aristocratic. My father's mother had a French influence on her cooking, which explained their rich taste.

Growing up, I could only spend time with my father's mother, and I loved having the meals she prepared for us. It was another opportunity for me to experience eating really good food.

We made these trips every summer, and I loved being around my grandmother. She was in charge of the kitchen. We would be served the same kind of food every day. My grandmother would go to the market and buy the ingredients. As a kid, I accompanied her to the grocery store, and she would let me pick things out. Filled with curiosity, I followed her around and observed how she dealt with everything.

This was a kind of routine I got into when I was spending time with my grandmother. I did this with her so many times that it influenced me heavily, to the point that I adopted the same routine in my life. To this day, I go to buy ingredients for the very day I'm going to be preparing meals instead of going for a big shopping list and stocking up on items in advance.

Our camp in Maine was on a lake, so we would go fishing every morning. Sometimes we would catch a fish and bring it home to prepare. Other times, we'd return home disappointed we couldn't catch any.

Every time I recall my summer memories, I feel a tinge of pain inside my heart, wondering if I'll ever get to relive those moments again. They will forever hold a special place in my heart.

After falling into the routine of daily cooking, I became more and more interested in the process. That was when I realized I actually loved it. It grew on me because of my mother and my grandmother, and they ignited my love for food and my passion for becoming a chef.

Apart from being around my grandmother, I spent the majority of my time with my parents back home. My dad worked till 6 p.m., and afterward, we all had dinner together. It was a lovely family ritual where we all sat at the dinner table together and talked about our days.

As I got a bit older, around the ages of 9 to 11, cooking shows started to air on TV. They had become a prominent part of our era, and I had so much to learn when I watched those shows. A lot of time, we turned on the television during dinner.

One of the top hosts of that time was Julia Child, so I watched her growing up. Another one was Martin Yan from *Yan Can Cook.* Watching these TV shows helped me develop a huge interest in food and cooking. Watching these professionals was therapeutic and compelled me to start my career on the same path as well.

Julia was a great influencer who taught me how to prepare meals and what it took to prepare delicious, wholesome food. While my family and I sat at the dinner table watching her, we had this simple ritual, or rather, a rule—we were required to eat everything. We couldn't leave anything out.

As a child, it was a great experience because it allowed me to taste everything, from vegetables to meats to breads and legumes. I was forced to try all kinds of foods. Fortunately, this was how my journey began.

Sometimes, I tried helping my mother with cooking and my father with breakfast when he made it every Sunday. Gradually, I learned how to cook eggs, make pancakes, waffles, and more.

In school, I wasn't a high-achieving student. I would get pretty average grades. At this point, apart from cooking, my interests also veered in the direction of sports. For four years in high school, I played soccer. I was a very good player, one of the best ones. I was also nominated as team captain, and overall, I had a great time playing soccer.

We also won divisional, county, and state awards. It was such an overwhelming experience. I loved every bit of my journey as an athlete. However, I somehow gravitated naturally toward cooking.

When I was 11 years old, my family met some folks who lived in Scranton, Pennsylvania, which was near the ski area. My father became friends with them and planned to take us there to ski. We stayed at their house for the weekend. We went to Elk Mountain for two days.

My dad went to Syracuse University, and when he was in college, he learned how to ski in northern New York. That's how he taught us to ski. It was an amazing experience.

All my life, I have had supportive parents who have pushed me to my field of interest and encouraged me to go after my dreams. They have been by my side all along and always encouraged me to do better. I'm so grateful to have such an amazing family and for our bonding, relationship, and everlasting faith in one another.

They have blessed my life in many ways, and for that, I am forever grateful!

Chapter 2
Formative Years

I knew I had grown up when middle school was finally over and I could step into a new phase of life. When I entered high school in freshman year and joined the freshman soccer team, it felt like life was going pretty well for me. I still struggled with my grades, though. I tried to maintain a C average. My parents were so busy with their own schedules that they didn't really see or realize what problems I was dealing with on my own. I was always willing to learn and perform better, which helped me. I was doing the best I could with academics and tried excelling at soccer too.

I was a good enough player, and I was always chosen to be one of the captains or co-captains. It was a great privilege to be recognized for my talents and get a platform to untap my potential. I was always the highest scorer on a soccer team, and I gained recognition in the high school league conference I played in, as well as in the county. I was also recognized in the state during my junior year. I was on the varsity soccer team and awarded an all-state New Jersey honorable mention for a left-wing soccer player.

But it wasn't all fun and games. I faced some pitfalls in high school too. I started smoking pot when I was wrapping up my freshman year. I was 15 years old when I was first introduced to marijuana. It was very prevalent in our town and in our high school. When I got to high school, its accessibility had increased. A majority of the students would always be smoking marijuana, even the athletes.

Even though I was a soccer player and a very motivated athlete, that didn't stop me from smoking pot. In fact, it helped me in my athletic practice. I found that when I smoked marijuana, it helped me focus on the practice I needed to do to become really good at soccer.

When I would practice, I really wanted to be the best one out there, so I got in the habit of running 4-5 miles every day. I found that if I smoked a little bit of weed before I started my run, it helped me focus on running. It helped me with my breathing during the run, which was the most crucial part of it. It retained my focus on keeping my mind motivated to continue running and meeting the five-mile distance I set as a goal.

I realized I only smoked marijuana because I was influenced by others around me. My friends and other kids were doing it, and it reached me too. Naturally, I felt driven toward it.

When I was 12 years old, my dad owned a manufacturing business. My dad asked me if I'd like to go to his factory on Saturdays and work on the production line to earn extra money. Prior to that, he gave me chores too. He would also give me an allowance if I mowed the lawn and took the trash out. He gave me 10 bucks, and I was always eager to make money through that.

Therefore, as a kid, I always had money in the bank. That's when I had friends turning me on to smoking marijuana, which also ended up with me buying bags and bags of marijuana. I discovered that if I bought a big bag, I could divide it into smaller bags and sell it. Now, because I had money, I started buying larger quantities of marijuana. I'd buy a quarter pound, divide it out, and create four ounces to sell three of them and keep the fourth one for myself.

Another activity that really excited me was skiing. I was gifted with opportunities because I did have money as a kid in high school. I had been involved in the ski club during my middle school years. And that continued through high school. By the time I had graduated from high school, I had taken many trips to the Pocono Mountains in Pennsylvania and also had ski trips with my family to Vermont. A lot of the time, this opportunity came because I had extra money in my pocket.

During my high school years, I would take a bag of marijuana, roll it up into a bunch of joints, and sell them for a dollar each. It was so easy because there were people who always wanted to buy them. I had my own little entrepreneurial thing going on, my own little weed business.

Another thing I got involved with in high school was skateboarding. I started in middle school, but I started to really get into it after I graduated. I was in high school when I got the idea to start a skateboarding business.

David was a neighbor of mine, and he was a surfer. We not only lived an hour from the Atlantic Ocean, but his family also had a place at the beach—the shore in New Jersey. We spent time skateboarding together. And I mentioned to him my idea about having a skateboarding business.

He brought it to my attention that I could do business through Surfer Magazine. There were companies advertising to sell wholesale skateboard products, so I decided to give it a try. I called one of the skateboard companies and told them I was interested in buying some parts and pieces to put together a skateboard. They agreed and sent me an inventory list. I could buy the parts wholesale, so I did that. I put my first skateboard together and started skating.

I had a few friends, and several of us started skateboarding together. I still had money in the bank because I'd been working from my home. One day, I thought, *why don't I try and start a little skateboard business?* I devised a strategy. I'd buy all the parts and pieces wholesale and put the boards together. Then I'd sell them for retail prices and make some money.

I started, and I felt like I needed help. I had a couple of friends, and I told them I would be starting a skateboard shop and that if anybody was interested in running it together, they could approach me.

I found two friends, Mike and Glenn, who were interested in the offer. They had some money because they were doing something similar to what I was doing. Glenn was a friend of mine whose parents were artists, and they really liked the idea. They decided that they would let us start the skateboard shop in their garage, and Glenn's dad built a countertop and created a space for us where we could build skateboards. That was what the 10th and 11th grades were like.

While I had so many interests, cooking was something that was still a top priority. We had an established rule at the dinner table—to finish all our meals. This led me to taste everything from meat, eggs, and veggies to all kinds of flavored and textured foods.

At one point, I started feeling averse to meat and the fact that it was a product of so much animal cruelty. I decided that maybe I would start eating a vegetarian diet.

My mom was the person who used to cook for all of us. When she found out I had made a decision to avoid eating all kinds of meat, she asked me to prepare my own meals. I did not mind the idea; in fact, I liked it so much that it quickly grew to become a beloved activity. I loved cooking, and this was one of the very first instances that showed me how much. Soon, I made my own fresh meals and loved the whole process that went into it.

When I graduated high school, I was looking for a job. My parents weren't so sure about me wanting to pursue a career as a chef, but they were still supportive. They knew I didn't do too well in school. I was an average scorer, but they didn't bring me down. They understood where my interests lay and didn't stop me.

I wanted to become a chef. My first job was at a wholesale bakery, where I was making pizzas. It was new, and I did not hate it. The experience was so nice because it made me feel like I could finally choose what I wanted in life. This was my first opportunity in the food industry. It was when I realized that I could see myself working in the food service.

Chapter 3
Secondary School Years

It was summer when I was getting ready for college. I had already been accepted at a small private college named Nasson College in Maine. It had about 800 students who lived on campus, located in the southern part of the state. It was right outside a town called Sanford.

The college was in a town named Springvale, which was twenty minutes over the border from New Hampshire into Maine, about an hour south of Portland, Maine.

I had been contacted by the soccer coach who was now going to take over the soccer program at Nasson. He introduced himself as Bob. He had been coaching the high school team in the town next to Cinnaminson, Delran High. He had won several state championships there and was ready to move up to coaching a college program. He had decided on Nasson, and he told me that I would have to report to school two weeks early for training. I agreed. We would have to meet a couple of weeks later in Maine.

So, there I was, getting ready to go up to college. That was pretty much about it, and I was looking forward to the new experiences that were going to be a part of my life.

One day, I was skateboarding in Cherry Hill, New Jersey. It just happened to be the biggest skateboard park in the world at the time. I had a membership. However, unfortunately, it marked the end of my skateboarding career.

I was there, skateboarding as usual, and I fell. I can still remember it so vividly. What happened was that I dislocated my elbow. Then I was rushed to the emergency center. It was treated, and the doctors ruled it wasn't a major injury, but my arm was put in a sling. I showed up to soccer practice with my arm in a sling. Apparently, it wasn't the greatest way to show up for my first day of soccer practice.

But it didn't bother me. I told the coach, "Don't worry about it, I'll do everything I need to do. In two weeks, I'll be out of this sling, and I'll be okay. And in the meantime, I'll do the practice. I'll run the five miles each day for practice and show up for all the drills. But I assure you I'll be okay." He seemed pretty satisfied with my attitude toward my team.

My first two weeks of college leading up to school starting were spent on campus with guys who were also on the soccer team. We were all living in the dorms. Soon, school started, and I had a full schedule. I had twelve credits, which included history, economics, math, and at least one other class. I don't exactly remember all the classes I was enrolled in.

I had decided liberal arts and environmental science were going to be my major. In college, my schedule was jam-packed; soccer practice was six days a week, and as a freshman, I was selected to be the captain of the varsity squad. My position was forward or left-wing.

We had a very successful season, and our record was twelve, three, and three that year. We were the best team in the Southern New England conference.

On a positive note, in that season, I was awarded the most valuable offensive player on the team since I was the second-highest goal scorer. I had scored a bunch of game-winning goals. I was the reason my team scored multiple goals. I even did a hat trick that year. In one game, I scored two goals effortlessly.

Soon enough, the season ended. Then came fall, and then, finally, winter. That was when I realized I needed money. My parents were paying my tuition. I was paying for my books and any other kind of recreational activities I took an interest in. Although I had some savings because my dad had let me work for him over the summer, I was running out of money.

We had a college dining room where 600 students had breakfast, lunch, and dinner every day. I went in and talked to the management company. I also wanted to work there. It was run by Ara Food Services.

I had an interview with the manager, and he agreed to let me work as a dishwasher. I took a job with the food service company in the college dining commons. As a dishwasher, I spent the rest of that first semester making at least enough to suffice for the time being.

In the second semester, I continued working part-time in the dining commons. At that time, I was also on the soccer team. Things kind of changed in the team. A lot of the team members had changed because it had included plenty of seniors, and they had all graduated, so the team kind of went into a rebuilding stage, and it wasn't nearly as successful as it had been previously. I didn't get the kind of playing time that I got the first year.

Academically, I was doing okay. I was hanging in. Before this, I had gone over and visited my friend, and we actually went to a Bob Marley concert in Burlington, Vermont. There were a couple of times I hung out with Tom at Plymouth State College in New Hampshire. We were keeping up with each other. Soon, he transferred to Colorado University for his sophomore year.

When spring break came along, I decided to hitchhike to Colorado to spend time there and visit with Tom.

Hitchhiking to Colorado was so much fun. It took me four days to get there. The road trip was pretty hectic because I was sleepless, had to keep waiting for the next ride, and was being dropped off on the side of the road. I had to hail every car and truck that passed for a ride. I was beyond tired. I had taken about eight to ten rides before I got to Nebraska.

I was stuck there for hours. No one was picking me up. Finally, I decided I was going to walk into town and see if there was a bus that could get me from there to Colorado. I had some money. As it turned out, there was a bus that was going to be coming through and leaving to go to Denver. So, I bought a ticket and jumped on it. I called my friend Tom and said, "I'm getting on a bus that is going to Denver Union Station." Then, he came and picked me up from the bus station. I spent two weeks at his house.

When I had to hitchhike back to college, Tom was generous enough to drop me off. It had started snowing really heavily in Denver at two in the morning. By the time he dropped me off, there was like a good six inches of snow on the ground already. He dropped me off on the interstate, under an overpass, so I could be out of the snow.

Within five minutes, the first car that came along stopped, and I asked the person where he was headed. He was going all the way to St. Louis. Call it my lucky day because he offered me the ride, and we headed off down the road.

It was snowing so hard. We made it to the Colorado-Kansas border. However, we got stuck and had to get off the highway. He got a motel room, and we shared a room for the night. The experiences I had just kept getting crazier, but I had fun while it lasted.

The next day, we drove on to St. Louis, which was an all-day drive. When it was starting to get dark, I became very uncomfortable with being on the road this late. He asked me if I had some cash on me and if I could be dropped off at the airport or the bus station. I liked that idea, so he took me to the bus station.

I wound up in Cincinnati, Ohio, the next morning. I got off, went out to the highway, and started hitchhiking again. A day and a half later, I was back at college. It was so thrilling. This was my first big hitchhiking experience. I had prior experiences, too, but this one, at the time, was the most adventurous one.

When I was in high school, I had certain opportunities that came up when I first started hitchhiking. My family and I would take these trips from New Jersey up to our camp in Maine. During those formative years, the Vietnam War was just ending. I must have been about eight or nine, and all these vets coming back from Vietnam were discharged from the service. When we would drive around to the East Coast, I would always see them hitchhiking to get around.

That's how the idea first came to me. I envisioned that if, at some point, I didn't have access to a car, I'd try hitchhiking too. Typically, when I got in trouble at home, my dad would take my car privileges away, so I had to walk wherever I wanted to go. That's how I started hitchhiking, which eventually led to this first big trip where I hitchhiked all the way to Colorado and back.

During my first year at college and prior to taking the hitchhiking trip to Colorado, there were three books I read called *The Teachings of Don Juan* by Carlos Castaneda, *On the Road* by Jack Kerouac, and Tom Wolfe's *The Electric Kool-Aid Acid Test*. After reading these books, I felt that there was more to life than what we were being taught in school and in a more general sense of the way society worked. My reading gave me a craving for travel and adventure. They were a big part of why I had no fear of taking on the ominous task of hitchhiking to Colorado and back.

But that year, soccer didn't go so great. We had a losing season. The second year, I was kind of losing interest in playing on the team, and the coach decided he was going to transfer, so that was going to be his last year coaching there.

The first year—two and a half semesters, to be more specific—passed by washing dishes. Cleaning the cafeteria area was also part of the job. Sometimes, it got tiring because the majority of students left a lot of stuff lying around, and we had to clean it up. So, I did that the first year.

Toward the end of that semester, I became friendly with a senior. She had spent the summer on the shore in Maine, working at a restaurant, and she was going to do it again that following summer. But she was a senior, and she was graduating. She ended up getting a job in her career path, so she asked me, "Hey, Peter, I'm supposed to be taking this job as a breakfast and lunch cook this summer in a restaurant called Annabelle's, and I'm not going to be able to do it. If you want the job, I'll tell them I have a friend who can take over my position, and you can go and work that job for the summer."

I agreed and ended up working. I also moved in with the same bunch of people she was going to live with while being on this job.

So, there I was, a sophomore in college, moving into this house that had five other people who were all graduating. I went down there, but I didn't have a car. I had a bicycle, and I had to ride it a mile and a half to reach that restaurant from the house we were living in. It turned out the place was owned by gay men, which gave me a very interesting summer. It was my first go at becoming a breakfast and lunch cook. I was in charge of cooking all the breakfast and lunch entrees.

It was my first experience taking a lead position in a food service establishment, and I really liked it. I had a great summer there. It wasn't a real busy place. We did 50-60 breakfasts and 20-30 lunches. I worked the summer there, and then I went back to school for my sophomore year.

That was when I got promoted to a prep cook job in the dining commons. One of the food prep tasks included cracking eggs. There would be a total of 450 eggs, but I was required to crack five to eight cases of eggs, which took about an hour and a half. I put eggs in both hands and cracked them on the side of the bucket. I'd drop the eggs into a China cap and then strain out the shells. There would be a four-gallon bucket of cracked eggs. Another task was heating the bacon and sausage, and then some of it was vegetable preparation.

I became really good friends with the guy who was in charge. He was a local guy. He was married and was in his mid-to-late 20s. We had good conversations about cooking and life. He would show me all the cooking he did, and I would learn a little bit about the cooking process through him.

During my sophomore year, I decided I wanted to transfer. I was going to leave Nasson College, and I applied to West Virginia University in Morgantown, West Virginia, because they had a really good soccer team. I called the soccer coach and talked to him. I told him, "I'm interested in playing for the team."

Coach was concerned with the fact that I had been playing on an NCAA Division Three team, and his team at

West Virginia was an NCAA Division One team. He also stated that all of his players were on scholarships. So, I requested him to let me come and try out for the team. I humbly asked him to at least give me an opportunity. And he agreed.

But what had happened was, I decided I was going to take a semester off and go back to New Jersey, live with my parents, and work for my dad for six months so I could earn more money and be in a better position when I had to restart school.

I ended up back in New Jersey, working with my father's business, which took me out of cooking for about nine months. I worked in my dad's factory that summer. And then, I had to go down to West Virginia to start school.

Chapter 4
The Grateful Dead

My life has been eventful ever since I was a child. When I was around twelve years old, I developed an interest in music. I asked my parents if I could have a guitar for Christmas, and they bought me one. It made me so happy, and eventually, music became a very important part of my life.

As I was growing up, I started listening to rock and roll music. By the age of 12-13 years old, I had already started buying my first rock & roll records. I bought an album by The Beatles and another by Bob Dylan, and I got the opportunity to hear a bunch of different San Francisco groups.

I went to my first rock & roll concert when I was fifteen, at The Spectrum in Philadelphia. I went to see Neil Young and Stephen Stills. They'd put out an album called *Long May You Run*, and they were touring. From the time I attended my first concert to the time I graduated high school at eighteen, I had probably been to ten different concerts, including Bob Dylan, The Grateful Dead, Electric Light Orchestra, Lynyrd Skynyrd, Bob Marley, and The Outlaws.

After I left Nasson College, I started working for my dad that summer. It was great to be back home. I was still very much engaged with music. Around that time, there was a

Grateful Dead concert in Lehigh, Pennsylvania, and my friends called me and told me to tag along. Tickets were sold out, but I decided that I would try to scalp for tickets at the concert. We made it to the show, but there were no extra tickets available.

Unfortunately, I had to stand outside the venue, waiting for my friends while they were in there, experiencing it all and having fun. I noticed a girl standing outside too. She had two beautiful dogs with her. I was tempted to approach her and tell her that her dogs were adorable. When I finally mustered up the courage to go over, I learned she was in the same situation as me.

We started talking. I told her my story, and we talked about all kinds of random things. I mentioned that I had been enrolled at West Virginia University in Morgantown. She told me she lived there, and it was such a coincidence. Here I was, abandoned outside a concert—well, not really abandoned, but kind of alone—and I met this amazing girl.

We exchanged numbers, and she told me that when I started school and needed a place to live, I could reach out to her. She would help me. Several months later, I was supposed to start back for the spring semester.

The girl's name was Susan. When I traveled to West Virginia before school started, I called her for help. I needed to find housing. She introduced me to her friend Eric, who had a family home he rented out. He was in charge of roommates, rent, and pretty much everything. I moved in there and got along with everyone pretty well. They were all amazing people and I got to form a great connection.

Susan and her friends had a Grateful Dead cover band. Eric was the leader of their band. He was the lead guitarist and main singer. Susan was a backup singer.

At the beginning of college, I was nervous. I knew I would be good at certain things and would find my way, but I was unsure as hell about other things. A new chapter of my life was starting, and I wanted to make sure I could navigate. I had to choose my classes, engage with people, and adapt to this new lifestyle. I was looking for clubs to join to keep me motivated and help me make my time in college worthwhile.

When I started the semester at West Virginia, I met the soccer coach. They had an indoor winter team I wanted to be part of, and I got accepted. I played through the winter on the indoor squad, and I did fairly well. I wasn't the starter, but they gave me playtime, and I scored a few goals.

One of the nicest and most fun things about living in Eric's house was that all the roommates who lived there were also musicians. They were not college students. Eric himself was a pre-med student. He was an intelligent and incredibly bright person. I'm so glad to have been friends with him.

When the semester started, I was clueless about shit. It was very difficult to keep up with everything, not to mention that I had gone from a small, private college of 800 students to a university of 35,000 students. I felt like a needle in a haystack. I had no idea what university life was going to be like.

I just got involved with the social part of college. I became a roadie for my roommates' bands. I would help them move their equipment around and attend all of their gigs. I tried my best to show up for as many as I could.

A big part of the social culture at WVU was drugs at parties. When I'd been in Nasson, psychedelic drugs were already a thing there. We'd have a big party every weekend. People would be doing LSD, mushrooms, and all kinds of drugs. Since I was an athlete, I had to be serious so I didn't get too drawn into it. However, I did try LSD. When I came to West Virginia, it was a lot of the same drug culture there too.

The Grateful Dead community was very into psychedelic drugs. The band had started off performing at a series of parties, mostly in the San Francisco Bay area, known as the Acid Tests. The parties were focused on the use of LSD, and the band would be present for musical entertainment.

The impact was great. The band felt there were no boundaries between them and the crowd and connected to their audience deeply.

I have been to several Grateful Dead concerts, but I was too naïve to really realize what was going on there. I got involved with this group of friends who were experimenting, and I kind of got drawn into it. This was around the time the semester was ending, and we were about to have a spring break. The Grateful Dead was coming to the East Coast for a tour. They were doing twelve stops in three weeks.

At this point, one of my friends told me that he and a bunch of his friends were following the band on tour and would be going to eight different concerts. They said I was welcome to join if I wanted to. I could hop in the van with them and go along. Of course, I said yes!

That was the first Grateful Dead tour I had ever gone on. It was a long tour, with consecutive shows lined up. Ever since then, it's been a lifelong activity for me, but at the time, the idea of going to more than one concert had never occurred to me.

We went to Norfolk, Virginia, where we attended two concerts. Then, we attended two concerts at the Civic Center in Philadelphia. After that, we went up to Syracuse, and later Rochester, in upstate New York.

The band played in Madison Square Garden in New York City, and Jerry Garcia did a solo acoustic show at Passaic Capitol Theater in Passaic, New Jersey. The last show was in Landover, Maryland, after which the tour ended, and we went back to college. We finished the semester.

Eric, who was a big Deadhead, had an opportunity to be a raft guide with a rafting company on the Cheat River in West Virginia. One day, he asked me, "Hey, you wanna be a guide this summer with the rafting company?"

"Yeah, sure, sounds great," I told him.

Rafting is an extreme sport. It is very difficult, dangerous, and depends heavily on collaboration. I was excited to try it, imagining all kinds of fun I had in store waiting for me.

When I went there for the first time, the experience was magical. The air was fresh, the water was crystal clear, and I felt a connection with the earth. During the trip, I could feel my muscles being worked out. It was exercise involving my whole body, and moving with the water filled me with a thrill that made all the effort worth it.

I could feel my heart pumping rapidly as the waves came closer and the tides knotted our boat. When I was training, I met new friends. We experienced a lot of challenging trips, but we learned good teamwork. We developed an understanding, and overall, we just had a really great time together. From splashing water and swimming to taking dives and racing each other, we had the time of our lives.

At the time, I had a Volkswagen bus I had purchased the summer prior to going down to West Virginia. We were using the bus to drive down to the Cheat River and do the training. We went through several weekends down on the river, training to become rafting guides.

Soon enough, I was qualified, but before I could even have a shot at that, I blew the engine of my Volkswagen. My vehicle died. I wasn't going to have transportation to get back and forth to the river. It was a sad ending, but my life has always been filled with adventures, which grew as time went on and I met new people.

I think life should be about your dreams and passions as much as about your academic or professional goals. It's important to have a good time in college, make friends, date people, and be open to new things.

College can be your spiritual and adventure awakening, where you learn lots of skills and practice how to manage a social life with work or academics. If you put all your focus on grades, you don't grow as a person. You spend too much time with books, and you don't know how to do things on your own.

I am forever grateful for all the fun and magic, in spite of the bad days. I know if I got a chance to do it all over again, I would!

Chapter 5
Hitching a Ride

My friend Sue told me she had a plan to hitchhike to Alaska and work there for the summer. She thought maybe I could join her. I decided to accept her invitation.

So, there I was in West Virginia, and the semester was ending, and my car broke down. Sue invited me to go on this trip to Alaska. She had a friend in Colorado we could stay with, once we made it to Colorado. And then there was a Grateful Dead concert too, which was going to happen in Berkeley, California. All the more reason for us to go.

Sue had a friend who lived there, and I had a friend who lived in Santa Cruz, California. I decided that instead of being a raft guide, I was going to go on this adventure and hitchhike to Alaska.

We made our plans, and we both packed our backpacks. I must have had 80 pounds worth of stuff loaded in there. Sue had a big backpack as well. We decided to take what we had.

I had a guitar and she had a mandolin. We both decided to take our instruments with us. She wanted to bring one of her dogs, Jazmine, a golden retriever, with us. It was the end of April, and our friends dropped us off in Wheeling, West Virginia.

Initially, the goal was to get to Colorado, then California, then Oregon, and then go over to Idaho. She was going to leave her dog in Idaho because she wasn't allowed to take the dog to Canada. And then we were going to hitchhike up into Canada, in British Columbia, up to Jasper National Park, and then all the way across British Columbia to Prince Rupert, where we could get on the ferry and travel up to Haines, Alaska. From there, we would hitchhike to the Kenai Peninsula.

Well, it didn't exactly work out according to plan. We started making our way across the United States, and a lot of crazy things happened. Eventually, we made it to Colorado in a couple of days, and then we landed up at Sue's friend's house. We stayed there for a couple of days and then went on our way from Colorado to California to get to Berkeley. We got to the Utah-Nevada border and got stuck there.

We decided to split up, and of course, the first thing that happened was a semi pulled over for her while I was half a mile down the road from her. She got in the truck and went off on her merry way, and there I was, left on the highway by myself, needing to get to Berkeley to meet up with her again.

It was another one of those situations where I was stuck on the highway for hours and hours and hours. I wound up walking several miles to the nearest town there. As it turned out, I could get on a Greyhound, drive all the way across the state of Nevada, and wind up in Reno, which I did. That was a 10-hour bus ride.

The next day, I made it to Berkeley. I made it there Sunday morning in time for the last show. The Grateful Dead concerts were there, and they were going to be held on Friday, Saturday, and Sunday. It was time for the last concert.

When I got there, I looked around for Sue, but I couldn't find her anywhere. I didn't have enough money to buy a ticket for the concert. It was at the Greek Theater, and right outside the Greek Theater, there was a recreational soccer field where the Grateful Dead had agreed to run cables. We could hear them for free from there. There was a whole set up of amplifiers so we could hear the concert on the soccer field outside the Greek Theater.

When the concert ended, I was speechless, as usual. It was an amazing show, and I had a fantastic time. Sue was still nowhere to be found. Finally, I realized I might still have in my wallet a phone number she had given me, belonging to a friend who lived in Berkeley. I called the number she had given, and she answered.

I told her I couldn't find her and that I was there. She came to pick me up and took me to her friend's house, where we spent the night. Then we decided to hitchhike down to Santa Cruz, where my friend was running an organic farm.

Once we reached Santa Cruz, my friend Francis agreed to let us camp at the farm. The only problem was, we were both out of money, and we still were a long way from making it to Alaska. Eventually, we decided she would go up to Corvallis since she had a friend there. She'd get a job, and I would stay in Santa Cruz and get a job there. We split up, and I stayed with my friend.

I took a job at a restaurant in Capitola Café. I worked there for a week, but things didn't work out for me. The restaurant served three meals a day, and my cooking skills were not polished enough to be able to prepare everything. So, I gave that up. I wasn't polished enough to be able to prepare everything.

The orchard was a two-acre parcel. The job was to thin out the apple clusters that grew on the trees. Each cluster had about twelve baby apples. I was required to remove about half of the apples in each cluster. To do this, you have to snap the apple from the stem, being careful not to snap the stem from the cluster. The work was a lot harder than I had imagined, but I had no choice. I would have to get through it in order to make it to Alaska.

You could usually spray the trees every season with pesticides. This stimulated the trees to naturally drop apples out of the clusters, but that particular year, they weren't allowed to use the spray because of the weather conditions. That's why I got hired to do the job.

The farmer let me pitch my tent because I had no money and nowhere to stay because my friend's house was twenty miles away from the orchard. I pitched my tent on the orchard, and I was there for three weeks. I lived on that orchard with a bag of bread, peanut butter, and honey. Every morning, I had to get up and put the ladders up against the trees. This went on for several weeks.

Finally, when I got to my last trees and completed the job, the farmer came down. He didn't come around that often. I knew I had to work until I got enough money to meet Sue in Corvallis.

The farmer told me I did a good job. Then, he drove me up to his trailer, up on his ranch, where we sat and had a beer and talked a little bit about life. Then he cut me a check for $400, which helped a bunch, considering I had no money on me.

My friend Francis picked me up and took me back to Santa Cruz. Then I packed up my things and said goodbye.

Chapter 6
Making My Way to Canada

The next day, I hitchhiked up to Corvallis, Oregon, and I met up with Sue at her friend's house. We spent the night there and were on our way to hitchhike from Corvallis over to Moscow, Idaho, where the university was. She had friends there, and the plan was that she would leave her dog behind because they weren't allowed in Canada. She would return to Idaho at the end of the summer to retrieve her dog. We spent the night there.

Then, we hitchhiked through Idaho and got off at the Canadian border. We were stopped at the border and our IDs were checked. After that, we checked out.

We started hitchhiking and reached about halfway up into British Columbia. We got our rides up to Banff, where the Canadian national park was. The last guy who gave us a ride offered, "Hey, I'll take you to the hot springs if you want to go." They had a beautiful, natural hot spring that ran through Banff, and it was right on the riverside too. We agreed, and he took us. We had a beautiful day hanging out at the hot springs. It was the most serene place I had ever seen.

We could see huge cliffs on the river and these big-horned sheep on top of the cliff. We were thousands of miles away from home, but we were living in the moment.

Soon, we left the hot springs and ended up camping in the woods.

The next day, we hitchhiked and went all the way up to Jasper National Park, which was even farther north. We hitchhiked all the way across British Columbia to a place called Prince Rupert. It was a port town just below Southeast Alaska. That was where we were going to get on the ferry boat. As soon as we got into town, we got picked up. We were still about five miles away from the terminal.

The men who picked us up were drunk. We got in the car with them, and they drove like lunatics. The driver sped through town like he was flying a rocket. He was running every red light. At this point, I was scared as hell. Sue and I looked at each other, reflecting the other's frown. We kind of signaled each other: *what the hell is going on?*

Eventually, we reached the ferry terminal parking lot. It turned out the ferry terminal was closed, and we had to wait till the next day to get on the ferry.

Since the terminal was closed, Sue suggested we go into town, and I told her there was no way I was getting into the car with those lunatics. So, we got into an argument, and while we were in the middle of it, those guys took off.

Sue got really mad at me and said, "Fine, you know what, I'm going to walk into town by myself." The town was still miles ahead, and I wasn't on board with her plan.

So, we split up. She asked me to return her tent, and I trudged back into the woods near the ferry terminal and slept in my sleeping bag.

Next morning, the terminal was open, and the ferry boat was there. I thought she would show up, but she didn't.

I moved along on what was now my solo journey. I got on the ferry. I realized I was running out of money. I had left Santa Cruz with $400, and by the time I got on that ferry, I only had about $25-30 left in my pocket. I didn't know exactly where I should be heading next.

Basically, the ferry traveled up the coast, past a couple of other towns, and then to Juneau. Eventually, it went up to Haines, Alaska. Part of the problem was, I wasn't sure exactly where Sue's plan was to end up. So, I was really confused.

I figured the biggest port between Prince Rupert and Haines was Juneau. I decided to wait there and assumed Sue would show up at the ferry port. I thought we would get back on good terms and start our journey together. Too bad that never happened.

For the next couple of days, I waited there, and each time the ferry would come in, she never got off the boat. She also never came into town. I never knew that after this split, I wasn't going to see her for another six months.

The day I reached Juneau, I realized I was very low on money. I didn't know anything about the place. I started talking to people, telling them I had just got there, was low on money, and needed help figuring out how I could plan to stay there longer or learn how to camp here. Someone told me about a state park where a river came down, gushing out of the mountains, and I could hike up into this park and camp there for the time being. So, I formulated this plan.

While I was in town, there was a big flea market in the middle of the town. It was kind of like a yard sale. I had a few things I needed to buy, so I decided to purchase some supplies. I bought a body suit of wool, long underwear, and some rope. Then, I moved to food supplies.

After I was done buying all the essentials, I went hiking in the state park. It was about a mile and a half from the park. I found a spot. I stopped by a tree next to the river. It had several wool blankets hanging up in it. I thought it was pretty weird, so I climbed up in the tree and retrieved the blankets. I got some extra warmth. Who would turn down extra blankets?

I continued hiking up along the river trail, and I reached this spot that looked like it had been a campsite before. I found a wooden pallet that had been left there, and I decided to build my teepee on top of it so that I would be off the ground.

I cut down a bunch of small trees and collected them. Then, I created a teepee. Since I had bought a tarp, I covered it with sticks and leaves. Then, I built my fire pit. So, now I had a small shelter I had bought and built, along with my little fire pit too. It was so exciting and thrilling, mostly to see I had accomplished it all by myself.

I started the fire and got warm. I ended up sleeping through the night, mostly because I was scared. I woke up the next day and went to town. I went down to the port, hoping Sue would get off the boat, but again, that never happened.

I was hanging out in the town, and I started looking for a job. There wasn't a lot of work available there because it just wasn't an economically developed town, and I wasn't sure exactly what to do. After a couple of days, I suddenly realized I was out of money, and I didn't even have enough for food.

Juneau, the state capital of Alaska, had a social welfare building. So, I got down to the state building and explained my situation. They told me the best they could do was give me food stamps. They gave me $100 worth of food stamps.

I thought to myself, *What a blessing.* That was going to at least help me with food for the next couple of weeks while I hunted for a job. So, I was going around to different businesses, knocking on doors, saying I was looking for a job. So far, I had been out of luck.

A couple of weeks went by, and I still hadn't gotten hired. Then, one day, I was walking through the woods back to my camp, and I came across a campsite with a couple of guys. I stopped by and started talking to them.

Among them was one person who had been in prison for six years for robbing a bank, and after getting out, he had become a survivalist, which meant he was homeless and was living out in shelters he had built. He was just getting by, by the looks of it. He showed me a poem he had written in jail. It was like a hundred-line poem, and I don't remember exactly how it went, but it was about being a survivalist.

When we really got to talking, I told him about how I was struggling and couldn't find a job. He looked at me and said, "Pete, I'm going to give you a little bit of advice. Part of the reason why you can't get hired here is because you look like a bum on the street. You got a scraggly beard and long hair. And nobody wants to hire you when you look like that. What I would recommend is, go get yourself a haircut, shave your beard, and you will probably get a job."

I went back to my campsite and slept on that. The next day, I went up to a beauty shop on the hill, knocked on the door, and introduced myself. I told her my story and said, "I'm out of money, and I'm looking for a job. I need a haircut; I need to shave, and maybe it'll land me a job." I told her I would return her favor if she just helped me with this.

She agreed, but first, she asked me to organize her storage closet. I got the deal, and by the next day, I started looking for a job again. A couple of days later, I got a job at a hotel. It was a small hotel, and my job was to take care of their lunch buffet. I was hired to take care of the salad bar and assist with setting it up. It was a twenty-minute walk from my campsite.

The one thing about Alaska in the summer was that the sun stayed up for twenty of the twenty-four hours a day. These were the longest daylight hours of the year.

I got a uniform. I would switch out of my dirty camp clothes and wear a uniform at the hotel. I was the new member of the team. It was a team of chefs. There was an executive chef and his assistant, and they both liked me.

I was starting to get to see it as one of my first opportunities as a professional chef in the industry. I was doing just fine; however, the job didn't last long. One day, I was told I had to be fired. I thought I had done something wrong, but it was just the general chef's order. The chef explained to me that it had been the hotel's general manager who had made the decision to fire me. I received a $500 paycheck, and that was it. It was still a blessing in disguise.

When I was in California, I had called my parents to let them know I was hitchhiking across the country. I had called them from California for the first time, and they thought it was crazy, but they let me do what I wanted. They just wanted me to be safe. I had been going around traveling a lot. Of course, it worried them.

During my stay there, I had sent a letter to my friend Francis in Santa Cruz. We had a high school friend that happened to be in Anchorage. Francis had told my friend Ron that I was in Juneau. Ron had sent me a letter with an invitation to move up to Anchorage.

I had enough money to buy a plane ticket to fly from Juneau all the way up to Anchorage. So, I flew up there and met my friend and his girlfriend. They took me over to his girlfriend's house.

This friend had found out about me being in Alaska through another friend of mine in California. That's why he sent me a letter. I stayed there for three days. However, I could only stay there for so long because his girlfriend's parents were out of town, and they would return soon. I was going to be homeless again.

I discovered a campground toward the end of town and realized I would have to camp out again and follow the same routine. I would camp and then go for a job hunt; I was scared that this was going to happen to me again because, once again, I was short on money.

Luckily, I got hired by a 24-hour diner—Flippers Family Restaurant. It was a chain of diners in Anchorage, and they hired me to be a grid—the graveyard cook. Soon, I started working in the restaurant, which was a late-night diner.

I was supposed to make breakfast, cook a few sandwiches, etc. By six or seven o'clock, it would get extremely busy. During this time, I was getting sleep only for half a day.

There was a lady who managed the kitchen there who kind of took pity on me. One day, she offered to let me stay at her place. She said, "Pete, I'm going to let you move into my house, and you can sleep on the couch." I took the offer. It worked out well for me.

In all of this time, I realized that during every one of my hitchhiking trips, one thing that always protected and saved me was praying to God. I have always had faith, and I believed that God was always looking out for me. Every time things got tough and I was waiting for a ride, worrying whether I would even be picked up or not, I had a firm belief God would pave the way for me. I would always say my prayers and have blind faith. It pretty much got me through.

I had moved into the kind lady's house, and I would crash on the couch. The setup worked great for me. I would take the bus from there to the restaurant.

One day, I met a girl on the bus who was pretty religious. She went to a church, and she discussed it with me. I was born and raised a Christian too, and it was easy to talk to her. We had a lot of common ground around our religious values.

I was drawn to this girl. I started hanging out with her group, who were members of the Church of Christ. Once, they invited me to start going to church services.

What started off as a really nice friendship and people to hang out with turned into a shitshow real quick. I was so naïve; I didn't know what the group I was hanging out with was up to. I would join them, but I didn't realize they wanted to baptize me. I had been baptized when I was a kid, but I didn't want to get baptized again. I wondered why I had gotten involved with these people in the first place. At the time, I went along with it, but it got super weird for me.

The months of July and August had passed. I finally called my parents and told them I was stuck in Alaska. Their advice was that since I had gotten myself into this mess, I was the one who had to get out of it too and that they weren't going to send me any money. I had decided to travel this far; it was my responsibility to get through the ordeal as well.

So, there I was, getting involved in this religious "cult", working at the diner, and saving money. The seasons were changing, and it was starting to snow in Anchorage. Around September, I had started worrying. So far, I had saved around $1,000, and I was wondering how I was going to get back to the East Coast.

At this point, somebody told me I should look in the paper, where people advertised if they were looking to share expenses. Hopefully, I'd be able to find someone to share a ride with.

I started looking and came across an ad for a guy who was looking to share expenses. He was driving all the way back to Virginia. I called him up and told him my situation. He agreed, and we carpooled the way back. We drove up to Fairbanks, into the Yukon Territory in Canada, and then all the way down the Alaskan highway.

It was miles and miles away until we hit the United States border. We reached the Montana–Idaho border, and it took us about three days just to drive down the Alaskan highway. We stopped at motels on the way down.

The Canadian Rockies constituted some of the most beautiful, picturesque scenery I had ever seen in my entire life.

Everything was good at that point. I felt safe. It had taken us about seven or ten days to drive from Canada to the United States and then across the United States all the way to Virginia.

So, I was still hanging out with the guy I had previously shared expenses with. We had crossed the Virginia border, and that was the end of the ride. I realized it would be better if I got in touch with Sue again. We hadn't met since our split and we needed to clear the air. I hitchhiked to Morgantown and showed up at her door.

When I knocked at her door, she appeared. We talked about our little fight and then easily forgot about it. I spent a couple of days at her house, and it was cool. She told me that after we had split, she started working at this cannery for a couple of months and saved money to fly back to West Virginia.

It was a nice, warm stay because we talked a lot. We shared our experiences and made up for lost time. One thing on my mind was that after this little encounter, I would have to go back to New Jersey.

While I was stuck in Alaska, my parents didn't think I was coming back, so they cleared out all of my stuff and moved it to New Jersey.

Anyway, I finally got there, showed up at my parents' house, and was excited to meet them after a while. I had missed them. They were obviously happy to see me, but they were also disappointed. I mean, I don't blame them because they were probably worried that I had kind of disappeared. Nonetheless, they were glad I was safe.

I needed money to survive, and I had run out of it when I got there, so I started working for my father's company.

But of course, that wasn't going to be enough. I needed to look for a second job, so I started looking at food places I could apply to. Luckily, I found a restaurant in South Jersey, in Cherry Hill. It was a very famous hotel, and I was immediately hired.

I started working there. I was enjoying my experience and was also making more money. I was lucky that my father had an extra car I could use to get to work. However, I was still living with my parents. It was a nice setup. The restaurant was ten miles away from my parents' house. I was hired as a breakfast and lunch cook.

I was working under an experienced chef who was an executive at the Philadelphia Club. He was in his late thirties or forties. He had been a very successful chef throughout the years. I had a great time working with him.

I would go in on Saturdays and then take care of the Sunday buffet, which was huge. After about three months, they asked me to join a union there. Apparently, it was a rule. I was against the unions, but I had to join it.

Right down that road, a brand-new restaurant was opening. It was called Bennigan's Tavern. It was themed as a steakhouse. It was a corporate restaurant, and they were opening them up all around the country. They probably had close to a hundred restaurants around the country.

It was a very well-organized system with a brand-new kitchen. I got hired there as a fry cook on the night shift. It was taking up a lot of my time. I went in there around three in the afternoon and worked until eleven.

That wasn't working well for my parents because I would reach home late, around midnight, and it really disrupted their sleep. My dad had to wake up early in the morning every day to go to work, so he couldn't afford to lose so much sleep like that. Eventually, they asked me to move out.

It wasn't too easy to get my own apartment, but luckily, I found one about a mile down from the restaurant. Dad wasn't going to allow me to take the car. He was letting me use it, so when I moved out, I couldn't really take the car with me.

I found a roommate who was also working at the restaurant. We were getting along pretty fine, and soon, we had a third roommate too. That guy was a proper pain in the ass. He used to sell crystal meth, and he would constantly bug me about it too. He would keep telling me random shit about it and would ask me to do it too.

The party scene was heavy there, and I was trying my best not to get too involved since I wasn't much of a drinker.

One day, I was drinking coffee, and I felt like it tasted different. I found out our third roommate had mixed some crystal meth in my coffee. I got pissed, and we got into a fight. We couldn't have it out at the restaurant unless we wanted to lose our jobs, but this was the turning point when I realized I wanted to get out of there.

I realized I wanted to go to Colorado. I wanted to move to the ski area, and because that was all the stuff I wanted to do, I didn't want to be in this environment of drugs and alcohol anymore. I had been an athlete all my life, and I wanted to get back to skiing and hiking in the mountains.

So, I went back to my parents and said, "I'm in a really bad place. I'll change jobs if you let me move back into the house for six months." I decided to save enough to go to Colorado. So again I changed jobs and started working at the golf course.

They had a clubhouse. It was a private golf course. The chef there was the director of food and beverage. He had younger Mexican guys working for him.

They were looking for a sous chef. At that point, I had about 4-5 years of cooking experience. I was hired, but I didn't tell him my plan was to work there for six months and then quit and move to Colorado. So, I got the job. This was more like a fine-dining restaurant.

The job was going pretty well. I was liking it, the chef was happy, and everything was going well. I had been getting to play some frisbee and some disc golf alongside too.

Finally, I saved up enough money, and fall was about to begin. November was usually ski season.

My brother and a friend of his had gone to Plymouth State College in New Hampshire. It was around the time the Grateful Dead concerts were also going on, so my brother talked to me and asked me if we could move to Colorado. He told me that when I was ready, I could move in with him. I agreed.

I had saved up enough money, and it was the right time of year. I called my brother. I wasn't sure how I was going to get to Colorado because I didn't have a car at the time. I found a company that needed people to drive cars for their clients out west, and they happened to have a car that they needed to be driven off to Colorado. This was how I ended up in Colorado.

I made it to Colorado and asked my brother if I could move in with him and start looking for a job and a place to work in Vail. He agreed. We started hanging out in Boulder. He was showing me around the town since he was a student there. We made a trip up to Vail. There was a ski event where they were hiring, and I got hired as a breakfast and lunch cook.

I had to start looking for a place to live. I started searching, and I found an area. It was a triplex owned by Johnny D. I paid a $500 deposit and moved in. It was about a mile and a half from the job. Time went on, and every week, I had three days off. I would go skiing on all my days off.

Soon, it was going to be summer, and I wasn't sure if I was going to get time to get any job that season.

I was either going to have to renew my lease or look for another place to live. One day, I saw an ad to find a job, and they were looking for someone for a part-time job at a pizza place.

So, I got a job working three to four nights a week at the pizza place, making pizzas and sandwiches. I took the opportunity. It was four days a week at the pizza place.

I grew up in New Jersey, and Long Beach Island was an island off the coast of New Jersey where I lived. I grew up about an hour away from there. I saw a job advertisement for Long Beach. I thought it was weird for a job in New Jersey to be advertised in Vail Valley. I called and went down for an interview.

I told the interviewer about my experience, and he told me, "You sound like you might be a pretty good fit for the job." However, they weren't opening anytime soon, so I didn't even know if I would ever get hired there.

Eventually, I ended up deciding to plan a trip to California after the ski area closed because we had some friends who were working on going there. We actually ended up going to San Diego.

It was a short vacation, but then, when I came back to Vail, I received that job in Long Beach Island that I had applied to. It made me so happy. I got hired as a sous chef.

I packed all my stuff up and flew back home to New Jersey. I moved back into my parents' house and told them I got a job on Long Beach Island.

I had saved like $4,000 from work, all winter jobs. This time, my parents were happy I had found a job near them. They knew I needed a car, and they supported me with it, emotionally and financially. I was finally able to purchase a Honda. My father and I each put up $3,000 and bought the car for about ten grand.

One day, out of the blue, an old friend called to tell me she was going to be working at Long Beach Island. Since we had an intimate history, she called to catch up. We talked for a while, caught up with a lot of things, and then she offered me to be her roommate. Now, I had a job, a car, and a roommate.

On my first day at the job, I met with the owner, John. He introduced me to a chef from Germany. Chef Rolland had worked his way around the world. He worked all over the place, and he was in semi-retirement mode. He didn't want to work year-round anymore, so he had taken this job because it was just a seasonal summer job. And he was the executive chef there.

The restaurant wasn't going to open for about two weeks. Because the restaurant hadn't opened yet, I was given an odd job, which was to peel a fifty-pound bag of onions. I felt like maybe this was some kind of test, so I went along with it. And for me, nothing was ever hard. When I got done with it, they were surprised, and I was hired immediately.

The place was a gourmet seafood restaurant, but it had a very casual atmosphere. They had 300 to 500 covers a day throughout that summer season, so it stayed extremely busy. I was in charge of managing 8 to 10 different employees and running the station on the line. The chefs really liked me. I worked from 11 o'clock to 9 o'clock at night. It was six days a week.

Long Beach Island had a beautiful view. The restaurant had a nightclub attached to it. It would open up around 10 p.m. and run till 2 a.m., with some live music occasionally.

It went very well. I had a great experience there. While I was living with Carla for the summer, I would go to the beach on my day off and party at night. I was having the time of my life.

At the end of the summer, I packed up all my belongings, took my car, and drove back to Colorado. I found a place to live when I got back in town. I went down to the Vail Associates' job fair and got the job. They hired me to work in another one of the restaurants. I was back in Vail.

Overall, it was a great summer. I worked hard, and I made a lot of money. They were paying me a good salary. I don't remember exactly what it was, but it was decent—probably around $35,000 a year at the time, but obviously, it was a seasonal job, so it had to end sooner or later.

I also applied to Vail Resorts with the ski area at the time. I got my ski job, which was going to be on the mountain four days a week with the ski pass.

Chapter 7
My First Big Experience Working in a Hotel

"Creativity is allowing oneself to make mistakes. Art is knowing which ones to keep."

-Scott Adams

As summer drew to a close, I knew it was time to leave my family and head back to Colorado, but before I left, I wanted to spend one last day with my loved ones. We shared a delicious dinner and talked about all the amazing experiences I'd had during my time away. They were thrilled to hear that I would be returning to Vail.

The next morning, I set off on my journey in my trusty Honda station wagon, which my father had helped me purchase. My first stop was my brother's apartment in Boulder, where I planned to stay for a few weeks to get my affairs in order before heading to Vail.

I was eager to return to my job at Eagle's Nest. As a grill cook, I knew this job was an essential part of my career and growth. Moreover, to ensure that I had a successful career, I attended a job fair at the Westin Hotel in the Cascade Village area.

It was there that I had the pleasure of interviewing the executive chef, Kevin. He was an impressive figure, five years my senior, and a graduate of the Culinary Institute of America. He had also completed a five-year apprenticeship at the Green Brier Hotel in West Virginia.

As I spoke with Kevin, I realized that working at this hotel would be an incredible opportunity for me to learn and grow as a chef. Without hesitation, he offered me a job as a cook in the café. I was thrilled to accept and eager to begin this new chapter in my career.

The culinary department at this hotel comprised specific areas dedicated to food production. These included the stock, soup, and sauce production area, which also housed the butcher station. Additionally, there was a cold food storage area, a bakery for all baking and pastry needs, and various food outlets. I would be working in the hotel's three-meal-a-day restaurant, The Café. The other outlet would be Alfredo's. It was a four-star Italian fine-dining-themed restaurant. The lobby lounge and bar, twenty-four-hour room service and a banquet department that was capable of preparing as many as one thousand meals per day.

As someone who was passionate about cooking, I was thrilled to have the opportunity to work in a four-star hotel setting. I was excited to spend the next four years of my career working there, from the fall of 1985 to the spring of 1989. Prior to this, I had gained valuable experience working in a variety of cooking positions, which helped me develop the skills I needed to advance my career.

Under the leadership of Executive Chef Kevin, the kitchen ran like a well-oiled machine. He had high expectations for his employees and made it clear that there would be no monkey business in his kitchen. Despite the pressure, we were motivated to give our best effort and produce top-quality dishes.

Chef Kevin was a master of his craft, with a particular talent for carving ice and constructing intricate gingerbread houses. During my time working alongside him, I found myself captivated by these unique skills. One day, I mustered up the courage to approach him and ask if I could learn from him and volunteer my time to assist with these projects. As the holiday season approached, I was eager to lend a hand in creating the stunning gingerbread houses that would adorn the Christmas buffet.

To my delight, Kevin welcomed me with open arms and generously offered to teach me his techniques. He did, however, stipulate that I would need to work on these projects after my regular shift had ended. Undeterred, I agreed to his terms and set to work alongside him, soaking up every bit of knowledge and expertise he had to offer.

Thanks to Kevin's guidance and my own dedication, I quickly became proficient in the art of gingerbread house construction, and when the time came to showcase our creations at the Christmas buffet, I felt a deep sense of pride and accomplishment in seeing our hard work on display for all to enjoy.

Overall, my time working in the culinary department of the hotel was an invaluable experience that helped shape my career and passion for cooking.

The café there had a variety of delicacies to choose from and people loved it! No wonder it operated all day long.

Being chosen as the lead cook for the café gave me an opportunity to create many new menu items I had never experienced before. Another great opportunity with this position was that I was in charge of ordering all the supplies required for the kitchen operation.

It took me some time to get used to the fast-paced work environment, but once I found my groove, there was no stopping me. I worked long hours, starting early in the morning and finishing late into the evening, but every moment was worth it. The kitchen staff became my new family, and we all embraced each other's strengths to deliver exceptional dishes to our guests under Chef Kevin's leadership.

From preparing elaborate banquet meals to whipping up decadent room service orders in record time, every day brought something new and challenging. It was hard work, no doubt about that, but seeing satisfied guests leave with full bellies made it all worthwhile.

To all my readers who share a passion for culinary arts, I strongly suggest a book that has been a game-changer for me. *The Professional Chef,* fourth revised edition, published by Van Nostrand Reinhold Company Inc. in 1974, is a must-read for anyone looking to enhance their cooking skills. This book has been instrumental in my growth and development as a cook, providing me with the knowledge and techniques to prepare a wide variety of dishes from the culinary world.

I cannot stress enough the importance of this book in my culinary journey. It has helped me master the art of cooking and has been a constant source of inspiration. Whether you are a beginner or an experienced chef, this book is a valuable resource that you should not miss out on. It will definitely be worth your time and investment.

The Westin Hotel in Vail was a four-star property and culinary program. It struck me when I learned that it was very classical in nature. It was an opportunity for me to be recognized as a part of the Culinary Brigade System, which was variously used in high-end hotels. I label it as a brigade system because its work is widely spread into various departments. I was intrigued by how each department had its own fancies and was elaborately taken care of.

From exploring the butcher's area, taking a close look at all the techniques practiced in the pastry preparation to peeking into the cold food production unit, I tried my best to pick up the best skills and practice them in my routine. Being hired in Vail would be a significant boost for my career and would aid in my progress.

Chapter 8
Bounce Back

Working in the mountains back then had its challenges because there were long breaks between the seasons. The ski season ran from mid-November to mid-April, and the summer season was from July to early September. Unfortunately, the new general manager didn't stay with us for long. The company decided to transfer him to another property in Washington, DC. Before leaving, he attended one of our kitchen meetings and offered some of us the chance to work at his new property during the off-season in May and June. It was a great opportunity for us to see how another hotel kitchen operated.

Upon hearing the offer, there were three of us who wanted to go; Shelly, Todd, and I. During this time, I had traded my Honda station wagon to switch it up with a Toyota Forerunner. We had a vehicle, my truck, and three of us planned to drive from Colorado back east to DC.

I was assigned work at the Manager's department there. The hotel got me housing with one of the chefs who worked in the fine-dining kitchen. John, my co-worker, worked at night, and his soon-to-be wife had a bartending job at a restaurant in the town. My shift, in particular, started in the morning and ended in the afternoon, so we rarely ever got to see each other. However, they were dearly kind to me and always willing to offer help.

One fact that I loved about being back on the East Coast was that I got to be close to my parents, close enough to meet and visit them whenever I got time. Usually, on the weekends, I would have time to spend some quality moments with my family. I would take my day off to set off on little getaways to escape my monotonous routine and work life. One of those weekends, when I visited my parents, I attended a Grateful Dead show at the Spectrum in Philadelphia. I drove up and went to the show first. After the show was over, I went to my parents' house and spent the next two days with my sister and Mom and Dad.

There was just something about spending time with family. It completely uplifted me and freshened up my mindset for the week ahead. My experience in DC was unique. One thing that I still cherish is all the skills I picked up from the Chef there. She was a very skilled carving artist, and I was keenly blessed to help her with a couple of pieces. I took the opportunity and learned a few tricks here and there with ice carving.

Ice carving was something I had initially done and learned from Chef Kevin back in 1985-1986. I continued it through 1989. I look forward to picking it up again in the near future.

In the winter of 1986, there were some unexpected changes at work. Chef Kevin decided to leave and take a job in Arizona. It took several months before a new replacement was hired. During this time, I went from being the lead cook in the café to becoming the Garde Manager Chef, in charge of the banquet cold food department. Kim and I attended regular meetings that were usually attended by the executive chef, which added a significant workload for me. As a result, I ended up working 53 days in a row, the longest stretch of work in my life.

Eventually, Chef Walter joined the team as the new executive chef. It was decided that the café needed a Sous Chef to handle its responsibilities, and I applied for and got the position for the 1986-1987 ski season. This was my first opportunity to work as a manager.

Chef Walter had a friend from Switzerland, Chef Daniel, whom he brought in to take over as the pastry chef. Chef Daniel and I became good friends. As the winter ended, Chef Walter also gave notice and left the hotel, but fortunately, Chef Daniel stayed. Another change happened when our general manager left and was replaced by Manager Mike.

After a couple of weeks, the new executive chef, Chef Chris, arrived. He was a fun-loving and talented guy in his thirties, with twenty years of experience working with the Westin Hotel Corporation. Chef Chris brought in several Sous chefs, leading to yet another shift in positions for me.

I was asked to become the assistant pastry chef, working alongside Chef Daniel. This provided me with a great opportunity to learn and improve my skills in the baking and pastry area of culinary art, with Chef Daniel becoming my mentor.

Apart from work, Shelly, Todd, and I would return to Vail for the summer. I would go back to working the garde manger position for the summer. I busied myself with the best of sports, soccer, biking, and climbing in the central Rocky Mountains. Climbing was my utmost favorite. From the dopamine rush while climbing the fourteen-thousand-foot mountains to enjoying the sense of achievement that came after, I absolutely loved the experience.

It was only the months of fall when it started raining and snowing. I remember a very dear friend had asked me to drop him off at the Denver airport. I drove him there, and then it was time to drive myself back to Vail. Little did I know a bigger misery was waiting for me.

It took only a few minutes to spin my life around. I got into a terrible accident where my truck spun around on the highway and hit the median guardrail. That was not just it; it flipped over the median and then rolled again, this time upside down.

It was the most horrific moment of my life. Lights flashing around, cars honking, and only my heart and head knew how I survived. I was extremely grateful to be breathing when I got rescued. Thankfully, there were no other cars that crashed. It was almost unbelievable that I had no injuries except the trauma that seeped into my head. I had been driving in the northbound lanes and would stop on the other side of the southbound. My truck, however, was in a pretty rough condition. It took me a couple of months to buy a forerunner.

After short turbulences, I finally reached the winter months of the year 1988. The whole year till 1989 was spent surrounded with good and happy times. I was working with Chef Chris, and I was almost learning the same stuff that I was already trained at. At that point in time, I didn't see my career excelling or prospering. It got me thinking about making a move in order to get where I wanted to be.

One thing I could think of was asking for a transfer to Seattle, Washington. It caught me by surprise that it got approved instantly.

Not long ago, before I moved to Seattle, the chef called me in, and we engaged in a conversation. He asked me if I was scared of flying in airplanes, and I told him that I wasn't. I had experienced plane rides before, and they excited me. However, I was really keen to know what he had going in his mind and what was going to be my next destination.

"I had won an award!"

As soon as the chef spoke these words, I instantly cheered up. Knowing Chef Chris and his work, I knew he truly deserved it, and I was so happy for him. I asked him for the details and how he would go about it. The chef told me he had won an award in a recipe competition. The Athens Filo Dough Company put on the contest out of Cleveland, Ohio. It was my absolute dream to win a prize in a competition. I was intrigued by his journey and looked up to him, so I was highly interested in knowing more.

He then told me that the prize they were giving consisted of an all-expenses paid trip to Cleveland for the weekend, where they would be holding the award ceremony. The prize also included a tour of the Athens Filo Dough Company, where they have their manufacturing plant and a city tour.

Chef Chris went on to explain to me that he had a fear of flying, and it was nearly impossible for him to go. He requested I represent him and accept his award on his behalf. At first, I was reluctant and didn't know how to react, but then I thought of Chris. I really liked him and his work. After considering it, I agreed to attend the ceremony.

The trip went better than I expected. I got to meet some well-known chefs who also attended the ceremony. Overall, the experience was great, and by the end, I was grateful that I had said yes to this opportunity.

The spring of 1989 was quite happening and life-changing to some extent. I packed everything and gathered the courage to move to Seattle, Washington. I didn't know what my decision would bring for me. However, I soon realized it was a terrible choice. I wasn't satisfied with my life there.

I was working in one of the restaurants in the hotel. The work didn't bother me much; it was the same kind of work I had experienced in Vail. I just felt really out of place with the staff.

Another factor that added to my dislike of Seattle was that I had lived in the mountains for the past five years, so it was comparatively more challenging for me to settle and adjust to city life. I only stayed in Seattle for three months, and my anxiety took a toll on me. It got to a point where I didn't want to stay even for a day. So, I decided to quit my job and return home to Vail.

Fortunately, when I returned, the room I used to live in was still available. I was grateful to return to my old roommates. When I moved back to Vail, I spoke to my friend Daniel, who had also moved back after spending some time in Utah. He told me that he opened a bakery in Avon, Colorado. Avon was just a city up from Vail. He offered me to join his bakery, but he wanted me to start in the early summer of 1990.

So, while I waited for summer to come and join my friends, I took a position at the Hyatt Hotel in Beaver Creek. The restaurant had more of an upscale fine-dining situation. I was happy to be working there, and the best part was that I got along well with the staff.

Ultimately, I was looking forward to working with Daniel the following summer. During the months of fall, winter, and spring, I worked a part-time job at the Vail Associates for the ski pass and at a cafeteria at the mountain top. Time passed quickly, and I had no complaints. My mind was set on a plan, and my future was mapped.

Chapter 9
Back and Forth

In the autumn of '87, as the leaves painted the landscape in warm hues, I found solace in the beauty of nature through my love for soccer, biking, and climbing in the majestic peaks of the central Rocky Mountains. However, one fateful day, while driving a friend to the Denver airport amidst snow and rain, my journey took an unexpected turn. My truck spun out of control, colliding with the median guard rail, flipping over, and rolling upside down before settling right side up on the other side of the southbound lanes. It was a terrifying experience, but miraculously, I emerged unscathed. Grateful for my life and mindful of the potential harm my accident could have caused others, I counted my blessings and, after a few months, was fortunate enough to acquire another beloved Forerunner to continue my adventures in the breathtaking mountains.

In the winter of 1988, things were going smoothly for me. I was working under the tutelage of Chef Chris, learning new culinary skills. However, despite my efforts, I couldn't see my career advancing much further, and I began contemplating a change. I decided to request a transfer to The Westin in Seattle, Washington, and my request was granted.

But just before I was about to leave for Seattle, Chef Chris called me into his office one day. He had a unique request. He asked me if I had any fear of flying on airplanes. I assured him that I didn't and that I had flown before. He said he had won an award in a recipe competition organized by the Athens Filo Dough Company based in Cleveland, Ohio.

The prize included an all-expenses-paid trip to Cleveland for a weekend, where the awards ceremony would take place. The trip would also include a tour of the Athens Filo Dough manufacturing plant and a city tour. However, Chef Chris admitted that he had a fear of flying and asked if I would be willing to represent him and accept the award on his behalf.

I was taken aback by the request, but I held Chef Chris in high regard and admired his culinary expertise. Without hesitation, I agreed to represent him at the awards ceremony. The trip to Cleveland was a unique experience for me, as I had the opportunity to meet and interact with other renowned chefs who were also present for the event. It was a chance to broaden my horizons and learn from fellow culinary professionals.

As I stood on stage, accepting the award on behalf of Chef Chris, I felt a sense of pride and accomplishment. The recognition and appreciation for his culinary skills were evident in the applause and congratulatory words from the audience. It was a moment that I would cherish for a lifetime, and I was grateful for the opportunity to represent my mentor.

The trip not only enriched my culinary knowledge but also helped me gain a deeper understanding of the art and science behind filo dough production during the tour of the manufacturing plant. Exploring the city of Cleveland, with its rich history and culture, was a bonus. The experience left me with cherished memories and a renewed sense of motivation to continue my culinary journey.

Upon my return to work, Chef Chris was thrilled to hear about the trip and expressed his gratitude for my representation. Our bond as mentor and apprentice grew stronger, and he continued to guide me in honing my culinary skills. The incident also inspired conversations among the team, and we exchanged anecdotes and insights about our culinary adventures.

In retrospect, I realized that sometimes, unexpected opportunities can come in the form of unique requests. It was a reminder that taking risks and stepping out of my comfort zone could lead to meaningful experiences and personal growth. Chef Chris' trust in me had not only allowed me to represent him at the awards ceremony but also opened doors to new learning opportunities and connections in the culinary world.

As I continued my culinary journey, I often reminisced about that winter of 1988, when a simple request turned into a remarkable experience. It was a chapter in my life that added depth to my career and left an indelible mark on my heart. It reinforced my belief that passion, dedication, and a willingness to embrace opportunities can lead to beautiful and unexpected moments in life's journey.

When I reflect on the events of my life, one decision stands out as particularly a bad one. It was the spring of 1989 when I made a choice that seemed a little strange at the time, but it ultimately led to a series of events that shaped my culinary journey in unexpected ways.

It all started with Chris, a fellow chef whom I had grown fond of. Chris had invited me to join him on a trip to Seattle, Washington. Despite some hesitation, I couldn't resist the opportunity to explore a new city and meet other chefs. So, I leaped and embarked on the journey.

The trip went smoothly, and I had some incredible experiences meeting fellow chefs and learning from their diverse culinary backgrounds. However, upon settling down in Seattle and starting to work in a hotel restaurant, I realized that it wasn't the right fit for me. The work was decent, but it felt like a repetition of what I had already experienced in Vail. Moreover, the city life was a stark contrast to the mountains that had become my home for the past five years, and I found myself struggling to adjust.

The time went on and I began to feel overwhelmed with anxiety. It was a tough decision, but I finally decided to quit my job and return to Vail, where my old roommates welcomed me back with open arms. During my time back home, I reconnected with my friend Daniel, who had moved back to the mountains from Utah and had opened a bakery in Avon, Colorado, just a short distance from Vail. He offered me a position, but it wouldn't start until the following summer of 1990.

So, while I waited to join my friend Daniel, I took a job at the Hyatt Hotel in Beaver Creek, where I worked as a line cook in an upscale fine-dining restaurant. Despite the initial challenges of starting anew, I was content with my work and got along well with the staff. However, I couldn't help but look forward to the upcoming summer when I would finally get to work with Daniel again.

One day, as I was chopping vegetables in the kitchen, a familiar voice called out to me. It was Daniel who had come to visit the restaurant. He beamed with excitement as he told me about the progress of his bakery and how he was looking forward to having me join him soon. Our conversation was filled with laughter and reminiscing about our culinary adventures in the past. It was then that I realized how grateful I was for the twists and turns of life that had brought me back to my passion and to the people who shared the same love for food and cooking.

I realized that my voyage was far from over as I stood in that busy kitchen, surrounded by the odors of sizzling pans and sizzling hopes. I was excitedly anticipating the following chapter of my culinary trip; however, with newfound clarity and a heart full of expectation, I knew that it would be even more delicious and meaningful than before.

Chapter 10
An Adventure in Baking

The vibrant colors of fall transformed into the glistering snow of winter. I eagerly sought out a part-time job with Vail Associates in Colorado. With a ski pass as my incentive, I landed a position at the mountain-top cafeteria, serving hungry skiers in between my exhilarating skiing adventures.

The days flew by as I carved my way down the slopes, basking in the breathtaking beauty of the winter wonderland. Soon the season gave way to the promise of spring; I knew it was time for a new culinary adventure.

It was a sunny spring morning in 1990 when I walked into the Columbine Bakery, eager to start my new job as Chef Daniel's assistant. I had known Daniel for a while, having worked with him previously at a hotel. He had started the bakery a couple of years ago, and I had helped him with some menu and recipe ideas during its early days. Now, I was excited to be joining him officially at his bakery.

As I entered the bakery, the aroma of freshly baked goods greeted me, and I couldn't help but smile. The bakery was small but charming, with white-tiled walls and a vintage vibe. Daniel was already at work, kneading dough on the large marble countertop in the center of the bakery. He looked up and greeted me with a warm smile.

"Good morning! Glad to have you here," Daniel said, wiping his flour-dusted hands on his apron. "We've got a lot of work to do today."

I nodded eagerly, ready to jump in and learn from the master pastry chef. Daniel had a wealth of experience and knowledge, and I knew that working with him would be a great opportunity for me to expand my skills in the world of pastry.

Daniel wasted no time and immediately put me to work. He showed me the different stations in the bakery, from the dough-making area to the finishing station, where the pastries were assembled and decorated. He explained that the bakery specialized in classic European-style pastries, such as Danish croissants, cakes, cookies, custards, and bread themes. Everything was made from scratch, and attention to detail was crucial in producing high-quality pastries.

I started with the production work, which involved making various doughs from scratch. Daniel patiently guided me through the process, showing me the right techniques for kneading, folding, and shaping the dough. It was physically demanding work, but I enjoyed the hands-on process and the satisfaction of seeing the dough transform into beautifully layered croissants and Danish.

After mastering the dough-making process, I moved on to the finishing station. This was where the magic happened, as the pastries were assembled, filled, and decorated. Daniel taught me how to create delicate sponge cakes, rich cheesecakes, and luscious icings. He showed me different techniques for assembling and decorating the pastries, from piping cream to creating intricate designs with chocolate and fruit.

While I worked alongside Daniel, I realized that pastry work was an art form. It required not only technical skills but also a keen eye for detail and a creative flair. Daniel encouraged me to be innovative and experiment with flavors and designs while also emphasizing the importance of precision and consistency in pastry making.

One of the things I loved most about working at the Columbine Bakery was the attention to quality. Daniel was a stickler for using the best ingredients, and he insisted on using only fresh, locally sourced produce and dairy products. He taught me the importance of understanding the characteristics of different ingredients and how they interacted with each other in baking.

One of my favorite memories from my time at the bakery was the day we made a special batch of raspberry-filled croissants. Daniel had just received a shipment of fresh raspberries from a local farm, and he was eager to showcase their vibrant flavor in our pastries. We carefully rolled out the dough, spread the raspberry filling, and shaped the croissants into perfect crescents. As they baked in the oven, the tantalizing aroma of butter and raspberries filled the air, and I couldn't wait to taste the final product.

When the croissants were finally ready, Daniel pulled them out of the oven, and we both admired their golden, flaky layers and the burst of raspberry filling peeking through. Daniel showed me how to glaze them with a light syrup to give them a glossy finish, and we eagerly tasted our creation.

The first bite was pure bliss. The buttery, delicate layers melted in my mouth, and the tangy sweetness of the raspberry filling was the perfect complement. Daniel's eyes lit up with satisfaction as he savored the croissant, and I couldn't help but feel proud of our creation.

Months went by, and I continued to learn and grow under Daniel's mentorship. I gained confidence in my skills and became more proficient in making various pastries, from intricate cakes with delicate decorations to simple yet delicious cookies. I also learned about the importance of time management in a bakery, as we had to work efficiently to meet the demands of our customers and ensure that everything was ready for the day.

Working at the Columbine Bakery was not always easy. The long hours, the physical demands of the job, and the meticulous attention to detail required could be overwhelming at times. But I was fueled by my passion for pastry and the joy of creating something beautiful and delicious with my own hands.

As time went on, I developed a strong bond with Daniel. We shared many laughs, stories, and creative ideas. He became not only my mentor but also a dear friend, and I was grateful for the opportunity to work alongside him at the Columbine Bakery.

Looking back, my time at the Columbine Bakery with Chef Daniel was a pivotal chapter in my culinary journey. I honed my skills, gained invaluable experience, and developed a deep appreciation for the art and science of pastry making. I will always treasure the memories of the sweet beginnings of my career as a pastry chef, and I am forever grateful for Daniel's guidance and the opportunity that he provided.

Chapter 11
Turnkey Restaurant in Eagle

I had grown frustrated by staying at the same resort for seven years. Life on the mountaintop felt transient and was not socially consistent. There were always people moving in and out of the resort, and I felt lonely. People would just come and stay at the hotel for the summer season and leave. At most, they stayed for a year and then moved, meaning I hardly made any friends. The job was socially unaccommodating, and I craved to live a normal life. I was eagerly looking to find a suitable place to settle into and was glad to have found the town of Eagle in Colorado.

In the Ski season of 1985, I had to visit a local county building at Eagle to register my car. It was the first time I had gone there; it was a town just 30 miles away from the resort. It had a small community of 3,500 people. The grounds were overlooked by large cattle farms and grazing lands for cows. Not to say that it was particularly an attractive town to settle into, but life there felt more normal than at the Ski Resort. The resort was a commercial center, and tourists visited it only on a seasonal basis. In contrast, Eagle had a permanent local populace who enjoyed their family life. It was easily accessible to other cities and had all government institutions. This compelled me to think about relocating here.

By 1991, I knew that I could not continue to work at the resort anymore and began to seriously consider moving out of there. I began to glance through the Vail daily classified ads to find a place to rent at Eagle. I couldn't buy a house at that time because my income was low and no bank would lend me loans. I even considered taking help from my dad, but he couldn't afford to purchase a house for me.

But I wanted to move to the town at any cost. One day, I came across an ad that had listed a Turnkey Restaurant for lease, and the owners were looking for someone to operate it. The ad was listed by a real estate agent named Larry. I reached out to him via his contact number and conveyed my interest in the place. He willingly volunteered to accompany me to the site. We went and checked the building, and part of the restaurant was already run by a lady, but the rest remained unoccupied. I immediately saw the potential the place offered.

At that time, the lady who was running the restaurant only offered breakfast and lunch four days a week. She only used part of the building, and the rest had once been a bar but now lay vacant.

Historically, the building was a house that was converted into a restaurant in the '70s. For a decade, the place was used by different restaurant owners who failed to see success, so it remained vacant for the next ten years until Wess and Rudy bought it. They tried to open a

Mexican restaurant but failed at it and eventually leased it out to the lady who ran the restaurant. But she was not doing well, and the owners were not able to pay the mortgage. They had been actively looking for someone to take over the place.

When Larry, the estate agent, took me there during the fall of 1991, I had told them that I would be busy working through the winters at the resort and they could reach out to me after the season ended. At the end of the winter, they called me and asked me to visit the building. I had grown tired of living on the mountaintop, and I always aspired to run my own restaurant. This was the right moment because the opportunity was knocking at my door. Without wasting any more time, I met the owners to discuss the possibility.

I tried to formulate a plan of acquiring it on lease. I thought I could use the capacity that remained idle and reopen the bar where it had once been, create a more suitable menu, and offer premium services. From experience, I knew I could cater to the various needs of the people in that town who looked for trendy food, and the town offered nothing other than classic food.

I thought if I could successfully do that, then even the unutilized space would not be enough to meet the demands of the locals. I wanted to move away from the conventional food that other restaurants offered and use my expertise to offer better food and service. I was eager to tap into a niche that was unserved and discussed it with the owners, who were delighted by my ideas. They encouraged me to find money and sign the lease and asked me to deposit rent for the first month in advance. But I did not have that kind of money, so I told them to grant me some time, and they agreed to it. I called my dad and asked for money, but he had nothing to offer. Instead, I looked into other places for funding.

When I was working at the bakery, there was a man named Pierre who worked with the bakery owners. He had a trucking business and took care of delivering bakery products to other restaurants and hotels. He had been thinking about opening a restaurant in Vail back then but did not have money to do so.

With the new opportunity in my hands, I approached him to invest in my restaurant. When I met him, we discussed the potential business, and I informed him that I had already done some groundwork and it looked lucrative. After a long meeting, we concluded that $20,000 was needed to start the operations. We agreed to set up a corporation in which each of us would be an equal partner, and under the agreement, I was responsible for running most of the operations, whereas he would be a silent investor initially. We approached Wess and Rudy and formalized all the paperwork.

Pierre was from Switzerland and had previously been in business with Michelle. He had studied accounting and had also been a ski instructor for 20 years. He was married to

Cathy, an accountant as well, so I thought both his wife and he could look after the accounts at our new restaurant.

Soon, we began to considerably plan about opening our restaurant. Initially, we struggled to come up with a good name for it and ended up with many names until one of my friends suggested naming it after my family name. I discussed this with Pierre, and he did not hesitate. I was delighted.

The cool thing about Pierre as a partner was that he didn't intervene with operations much and allowed me to be fully in charge. I was glad about it because I did not like other people telling me how to run my restaurant, and from both our experiences, we knew that if two people were looking over operations, then conflicts were bound to rise, and it was best for him to focus on what he had been good at—ensuring smooth supplies to our customers and keeping an eye on our accounts. This did not mean I was not aware of the financial position of the restaurant. On the contrary, I would hold frequent meetings with Pierre to ensure accounts were run smoothly.

Honestly, running the restaurant hurt us financially for three years. We lost money every month, and our expenditures always exceeded our income. It was hard to keep the business running, and our customer base did not grow by large. Then, the maintenance costs began to rise. A refrigerator or a cooler would break now and then. We also had to put on new carpets and repaint the building. Some of these expenditures were unexpected, but we kept on serving our customers. Eventually, we ran out of cash and had to loan some money out of the bank. At that time, the support I got from Pierre was instrumental, and he was diligently working to reduce the damage already done to our cash flow. It was a lot of hard work from him, and it was not until the 37th month of operations that we finally began to generate profits for the first time.

Nonetheless, I was glad to have become a restaurant owner. It took me a lot of years of working under different bosses to finally open my restaurant on the 3rd of August, 1991. Though still new, the restaurant was well-received by the townsmen. We were grateful for our friends and the families in the country who frequented our restaurant and spent their time and money. It was not just for lunch or dinner that they would visit our restaurants; at times, the locals would just sit there and enjoy a coffee and share their experiences with us. Some old customers had lived in the town for 50 years and had interesting stories to tell us. It was a great time in my life, and I loved the struggle of those years and still remember it with fondness. I am deeply grateful to the people, my family, and Pierre for staying with me through some of the hardest years of my life.

That year, I lost Pierre as my partner because he chose to get out of the business. He had an opportunity to take ownership of Michael's bakery and decided to make the most of it. I missed his presence because, for seven years, he had been with me at the restaurant and helped me manage the finances. We used to meet every week when he delivered bread to the restaurant and collected the invoices. He was a handyman and also helped with maintenance work. Together, we managed to run the business in some of its most difficult years. Now that he was gone, I was pretty much on my own running the restaurant, but I was glad to have him alongside me and wished nothing but the best for Pierre as he embarked on a new journey.

Chapter 12
Brenner Family Restaurant

As a proud owner of a restaurant, I felt ecstatic to have all my hard work and struggles of the last few years pay off. Though I was over the moon with my ownership, little did I know that operating a restaurant would prove to be chaotic. Stepping into the role of executive chef and general manager brought huge responsibilities.

I was required to look over most of the operations at the restaurant and ensure customers didn't face any issues while enjoying their meals. This was a staggering jump in my career and made me nervous. Indeed, the scope of my responsibilities had increased tenfold.

We planned to open the restaurant in early August 1991. However, it took us some time to renovate the restaurant to our liking. The exterior of the restaurant required repainting, while the interior needed a little more than just repainting. The carpets on the floor needed replacement. I also had to renovate the bar to make it suitable for our customers. We also added a pick-up window for food services in the kitchen, built new counters, and finally attached a steam table. It was a lot of work, and I felt indebted to my roommate for his efforts in helping me open the restaurant on time.

Thankfully, most of the preparations were in order, and it didn't take us long enough to start our operations. I had already prepared the menu for my restaurant and set up agreements with suppliers. They cooperated with me to ensure timely deliveries.

Pierre looked after payroll, accounts, and taxes. While that side of the business was sorted, we still had a lot on the other side—the front. We had to hire new people and needed a solid crew to back up our services. I had to diligently ensure that we employed the right people, especially because our line of business relied on making a positive start. So, I started small and hired a small team of hard-working people.

Initially, it started with Craig, Tammy, and Riva. They helped me prepare food in the kitchen and also assisted with serving our customers. However, during lunch hours, things began to get chaotic as the restaurant was usually full of customers, and it was hard to manage by a few people. I discussed it with Pierre, and we agreed to hire another cook who could prepare meals for lunch. Still, it was hard to manage because we had to prepare at least 60 meals on a typical day. So, we had to hire even more people. Eventually, the crew grew to eight people. Even then, I had to step in. I remember struggling every day between the kitchen and the dining room, serving the unattended customers with food.

There was a lot of construction work going on at Eagle back then, so I would receive many workers at lunch hours, which usually made my restaurant buzz. The county was home to various government buildings where a lot of officials worked. Most of them frequented my restaurant for lunch, and I was happy to see so many customers flocking in. We expanded our operations and opened for seven days a week and closed the restaurant on Sundays only.

This meant more work for me. I was responsible for cooking dinner for all six nights of the week. Then, I had to clean all the utensils, which included all the pots, pans, and other kitchen equipment. It was a tremendous amount of work, and I used to get exhausted by the end of the week. It wasn't just physically demanding, but once I was done working inside the kitchen, I had to make so many decisions that it used to suck all the energy out of me.

A typical day at work started early in the morning. I woke up while the rest of the town was still sleeping. It used to be dark outside when I would drive to the restaurant. It was only a quarter mile away, and once I reached there, I would check up on my dog, Czar. I would run through the stock of supplies to make sure they were maintained at the right temperature. Then, I would take a tour of the kitchen to ensure everything was in order.

By the time banks had opened, I would take money from the cash register and deposit it in our joint account at the bank. After returning from the bank, I would stop at the local grocery store, Beasleys, to buy supplies for my restaurant. I liked the store because it was small, yet had everything I needed for the restaurant. Then I would get back to the restaurant where supply trucks would already be dispatching the supplies for the day. As the deliveries were offloaded, I would chat with the truck drivers as I loved talking to them. They were fun and always shared interesting stories from their driving adventures.

Once the drivers went on their way, I would check the list of items to ensure deliveries were accurate. Then, I would proceed to generate the invoice. This was my favorite part of my day because receiving the products made me happy; I felt great joy in receiving the supplies that I was going to use for cooking. These were the little moments that meant a lot to me.

Another challenge that I faced while setting up the 'Brenner family restaurant' was getting a liquor license. Back then, the state authorities needed to approve a restaurant if it wanted to serve liquor to its customers. It used to be a lengthy process, and it took us several months before the license was approved.

However, there was another challenge waiting for us. I had no prior experience working at a bar, and I wasn't sure if I was the right fit for this job. However, I loved the restaurant and was willing to learn anything to ensure it ran successfully.

So, I began serving the customers alcohol when they ordered their meals. Once I learned a bit more about the business, the restaurant generated profits for the first time in a few months. In the long run, we relied on money generated from liquor to survive some of the most daunting years of running the restaurant.

Besides cooking, I was always interested in playing golf. When I moved to Colorado, I shared this interest with many of the locals. At times, I participated in disc golf competitions and enjoyed it more than regular golf. I participated in various tournaments every year in Denver and other areas of Colorado. Then I got to know a lot of people who had an interest in disc golf and took part in the competitions. I loved these competitions and soon became a member of the Colorado Disc Golf Association. With this, I also joined the Professional Disc Golf Association (PDGA).

Back then, there were no disc golf courses in the central Rocky Mountain region. So, I made it a point to make one on my own. There was a large terrain of land behind my house that was owned by the county. It was an old ranch along the Eagle River, basically lying useless for many years. I thought it was the perfect place for making a disc golf course.

While reading through the PDGA magazine, I got to know that a worldwide event for disc golf was being organized. It was sponsored by a local company, Circular Productions, based in Texas. The idea behind the event was to ensure a maximum number of people played disc gold over a weekend scheduled in May. If anyone signed up for the event, the sponsoring company would provide all the participants with T-shirts and discs. Then, there would be a prize of nine-disc golf baskets, and it was awarded to the town which gathered the maximum number of participants.

I quickly went to the county officials and requested them to allow me to use the land beside the Eagle River for the event. I was glad when they agreed to it. I bought 18 reflector poles and sat a course on the proposed land. Next, I had to create awareness about the event.

Previously, I had worked with the local radio station to conduct marketing events for the restaurant, and when I informed them about my plans, they willingly donated slots that spread over several weeks. I felt happy because I was able to get the word out to the whole town about the event. The marketing stunt worked, and the event turned out to be a great success. By the end of the weekend, we had more than 90 participants.

I shared all the details of the tournament with our sponsors, Circular Productions. John, the owner of the company, informed me that Eagle had the best results for the tournament. This meant our town managed to get more participants than any other town ever could. We were crowned world champions of the event and were pleased to receive the nine baskets. This was a proud moment for me and I was filled with immense joy.

There was one last thing that needed to be done—get the nine-disc golf baskets. For that, I needed approval from the authorities at the county to grant this land for playing golf so that I could place the nine baskets on the Fair Grounds Property beside the river. The authorities permitted the use of land for golf, and that is how I started the first Disc Golf Course in the central Rocky Mountain region. From then on, I hosted professional disc golf competitions every year for the next eight years.

With time, the county of Eagle grew, and I saw a change happening around me. Many new restaurants opened and that took most of our customers away. This hurt us financially, and we kept on losing money for over a year.

By 1999, the losses drained us of our savings, and continuing the business looked risky. I talked to Rudy and Wess and told them about the loss the restaurant was going through. I also informed them that we would not be able to renew our lease as it was going to expire by the end of that year. They understood and agreed when I suggested closing the restaurant. Sadly, I had to abandon my dream and look for opportunities elsewhere.

Chapter 13
Meeting My Love

The closing of my restaurant was a massive blow, and I was incredibly disappointed. It was a lifelong dream to become a restaurant owner, and when I finally achieved it, I was relieved to be free from the constraints of working for others. Curating a menu and providing my customers with top-quality, hygienic food was incredibly rewarding, as was the utilization of the vacant space to offer a selection of exceptional wines.

Initially, the restaurant did incredibly well, but as new competitors entered the market, our customer base dispersed, which hit our cash flow. It was a depressing time, and as our financial situation deteriorated, Pierre had no option but to suggest closing the restaurant since it was no longer sustainable to continue.

It took me an additional two weeks to move all the equipment and tools out of the restaurant after we closed. I moved them to my garage at Eagle Villas Apartment Complex, where eventually my wife and I lived. Despite the difficult time, my wife was incredibly supportive, and she motivated me to seek out other job opportunities, for which I'll always be grateful.

I had relocated to Eagle for a fresh start and quickly developed a fondness for the town. The residents were closely connected and hospitable, making it easy to make new friends as I familiarized myself with the surroundings. During my routine drives, I spotted an attractive woman working as a landscaper near a hill. Over the next few weeks, I noticed her several times and became increasingly fond of her.

Luckily, the woman I saw on the hillside visited my restaurant with one of her coworkers during lunch hours. During that time, I hired assistants who helped me prepare the food, which gave me more time to spend in the restaurant, greeting my customers. If the assistants needed my guidance, they could call me, and I would step into the kitchen to ensure everything was running smoothly.

I was excited to see her and helped them settle at a table. It was a busy day at the restaurant, and the waiters were dealing with other customers, so I ended up taking Anne's order. When I reached her, she asked for something that was not on the menu: a tuna sandwich. If it was some other customer, I would have simply directed them toward another item on the menu, but since it was her and I wanted her to stay, I decided to take her order with a smile.

I knew there was tuna in the inventory, so I quickly headed into the kitchen and carefully prepared her a sandwich. She was elated because her sandwich was delicious.

After she had her sandwich, we sat there and chatted for a while. It was our first meeting, and we hit it off very well. I liked her. She lived in an apartment nearby, which meant we could see each other more. One day, I rode my bike to her house and we talked for a while. She had been married for a few years and had two sons. However, things hadn't been so easy. Her marriage was on the verge of breaking apart, and she had filed for divorce. When I asked her if she was interested in going on a date with me, she declined the request because she had too much trouble going on in her life. I empathized with her and offered her the space and time she needed.

By September of that year, her divorce was finalized. After that, I kept on calling her and asking her out on a date but she was persistently hesitant. After a few weeks, she visited me at the restaurant and invited me to a party that she was attending with her sons. I was thrilled and could not believe that she had finally agreed to go out with me. I accepted her invitation and we went to a house in the valley. It was the birthday party of one of the kids who were friends with her sons. There were a lot of families, and I enjoyed my time with Anne and her kids.

The house had a pond in the backyard, which was the highlight of the entire party. The kids enjoyed getting their clothes wet and dirty in it. When her sons, Luke and Brady, got back, they were drenched in muddy water. I helped them clean up and tried to get to know them better. They were polite and welcoming.

During that time, the restaurant was not doing well financially. The profits fluctuated every month and we barely managed to keep it running. Our customer base varied on a seasonal basis. The locals could not afford to dine out frequently, so we depended on the tourists who visited the town in the summers and winters, and that affected my business greatly.

I discussed my financial troubles with Anne, and she was still willing to stay with me. We continued to date for several years and loved spending time with each other. I looked after her sons, and she was willing to assist me both emotionally and mentally. Whenever I faced problems with my business, she volunteered to support me. I knew she was going to be a great partner.

On the 24th of December, 1997, we got married. At that point, Luke and Brady were 10 and 12 years old, respectively. Following our union, my spouse assisted me in operating our restaurant business. She would take on various roles, such as serving customers by taking their orders or handling the financial aspects by managing the accounts. Meanwhile, I focused on maintaining and cleaning the restaurant and had to dedicate extra hours on the weekend to look after the restaurant.

Though we tried hard to keep the eatery running, we faced significant financial setbacks, due to which our restaurant was shut down. This was an incredibly difficult period for me as I struggled emotionally and mentally. The dream of running my restaurant came crashing down.

However, during that time, I discovered that Anne was a much stronger woman than I initially thought. She committed to supporting me in every way, including financially, and even took up a position as a ticket agent at the local airport. This provided temporary relief from my financial concerns, allowing me to focus on exploring new opportunities for my career growth.

Chapter 14
Back to the Hotel Industry

After my time at the restaurant, I eagerly accepted my first job at the renowned Marco's Pizza, located in Gypsum, Colorado. This charming little town was situated merely 8 miles away from my residence in Eagle. I had gained substantial experience working at other pizza joints earlier in my career, and it didn't take long for me to realize that returning to the world of pizza-making was not just a convenient option but also a passion-driven one.

The entire process of crafting a scrumptious pizza seemed like an intricate piece of art—from diligently mixing ingredients for the perfect dough to meticulously simmering the flavorful sauce. However, the real excitement began when I started stretching out the dough and generously smothering it with toppings before sending it on its journey through the fiery oven. And who could forget the finishing touch—expertly cutting it into uniform slices and adding my personal touches to it.

My responsibilities at the pizza joint didn't end there; I often found myself on the other side of the counter, manning the cash register and building rapport with our loyal customers. All in all, this job turned out to be an amazing experience where I honed both my culinary and interpersonal skills.

Further, the journey ahead continued with an interesting mix of tasks and responsibilities. This initial job was a brief experience, lasting just four months before I moved on. Next, I found myself employed at another restaurant, which, of all places, took me back to Eagle County—a place that was home to me. Hard to believe, but this new restaurant was the previous top competitor to my restaurant! Forgetting about the past ordeals, I took on the role of Executive Chef, hoping to do a good job there.

However, it wasn't long before I discovered that the restaurant was on the market and due to be sold. Despite my enthusiasm for this position, it only lasted for another four months before the establishment changed hands. Unfortunately for me, the new owner had already selected a chef for their new restaurant, and once more, I found myself searching for employment in the culinary world.

During the vibrant autumn of 2000, I was thrilled when renowned Chef Todd hired me to serve as his dedicated sous chef at the prestigious four-star hotel restaurant CHAPS Chop House. Renowned for its exquisite culinary offerings, CHAPS catered to a distinguished clientele for both lunch and dinner services. The restaurant's distinguished menu featured delectable steaks, succulent chops, fresh seafood, and an array of classic items that complemented the chop house theme. My tenure as sous chef extended until the blossoming spring of 2001. Upon the conclusion of the exciting winter season, the hotel's management identified my talents and promoted me to the esteemed role of Banquet Chef.

In my new role, I found myself primarily responsible for serving the diverse range of guests who attended various events at the hotel. Our extensive menu catered to all tastes, boasting a plethora of appetizers, sumptuous soups, and a range of mouth-watering hot entrées, all prepared under my supervision.

The number of attendees at these events varied greatly; I found my team serving as few as 10 intimate diners to grand gatherings of up to 800 guests. This diverse customer base certainly presented its own set of challenges, pushing me to constantly refine my culinary skills. I found the whole process challenging—from mastering the art of butchering delicate meats and seafood to testing my creative potential at preparing a variety of vegetable dishes. However, I embraced this part wholeheartedly.

One task I particularly relished was preparing the delectable Demi-Glace sauce. Simmering in a massive 80-gallon kettle over three long days, the entire process demanded a lot of precision and patience. But ultimately, the rich flavors and universal appreciation for this sauce made each painstaking moment completely worthwhile.

Unfortunately, Chef Todd left the hotel in 2002 and went on to open his restaurant. In 2003, I decided to take up a temporary position at a Gold Course Country Club for the summer. This was with the Cordillera Valley club, and I would run their restaurant that was called The Chaparral. I loved working there and serving all the members. This job was a lot less demanding than my previous job at the Banquet Hotel.

As I reflect on my early days in the hospitality industry, I vividly remember the long hours I put in as a full-time employee at a steak-themed restaurant serving both lunch and dinner. Although it was challenging, the job did come with a few perks, such as access to the golf course. I loved playing golf and, needless to say, I spent most of my summer days on the green.

Once summer came to an end, I returned to my former position as garde manger at the hotel. I was back in the swing of things, focused and determined to move up in the kitchen. For the next six years, I worked as a Banquet Chef, but this time, I had a cooler job, as I was in charge of preparing a variety of cold dishes. It was still not an easy task catering to hundreds of people, but it was far more manageable than working on the hot side because the cold dishes could be prepared ahead of time and didn't require much maintenance.

I recall having a team of three assistant chefs to help me prepare all the food. Despite the long hours, I enjoyed every minute of working under the meticulous supervision of four executive chefs: Mike, Werner, Randy, and Richard.

During my six years of working with my talented colleagues in the culinary field, I consistently received unique and innovative ideas for preparing dishes, which helped me to learn and grow as a professional. Although I had hoped to obtain the role of Pastry Chef, I was transferred to the bakery department instead. I didn't work at the bakery department and ultimately returned to work as the garde manger where I continued to apply the skills and knowledge I gained from my colleagues.

Chapter 15
Finding Our Nest

The year 2003 marked a turning point in my life. Three vital aspects of my life were moving in the right direction, creating a sense of alignment and fulfillment that was nothing short of incredible. My career had finally found some stability. Secondly, my financial situation had improved considerably, and most importantly, my incredible partner Annie and I were charging full steam ahead, working hard to build a life together.

I'd been juggling multiple jobs for quite some time— the kind of backbreaking labor that instills a deep appreciation for every hard-earned dollar. During that time, I managed to secure a stable position. This new job not only provided me with financial stability but also allowed me to save money.

Having been scrupulous with my spending and savings habits, I watched as my bank account swelled slowly but steadily, finally allowing me some breathing room after years of facing losses at my family restaurant. The newfound stability offered a beacon of hope, and for the first time in a few years, I could afford some luxuries— or at least ponder the idea of spending on non-essentials without feeling a pang of guilt or stress.

At that time, my wife had also been supportive and was frugal with money. To support our household, she started working at the county airport as a ticketing agent. She did her job with utmost dedication and fulfilled all her duties religiously. Her bosses were pleased to have her, and I appreciated her financial input into our household. Together, we had come to rely on each other's support during challenging times, and our mutual commitment to our dreams and aspirations only served to strengthen our bond.

During that time in our lives, our family's financial status had finally improved, allowing us to look for a suitable house that we could call our own.

As luck would have it, the government had started a housing program for the county of Eagle called Deed Restricted Housing; it was specifically designed for people like us. This was a program that made it possible for the working class to acquire affordable housing and attain their dreams of homeownership. We had to prove our residency in Eagle County and provide evidence of our employment status to be considered for access to this type of housing. It was a rigorous process, but the reward was worth the effort. It marked the start of our journey toward building our dream home. Looking back, I am grateful for the opportunity that was presented to us, and I know that it has played a significant role in helping my family find a permanent place to reside in.

Anne and I managed to satisfy the primary criteria as we were employed full-time and were earning sufficient money. That made us eligible to join the program. At the time, I was seeking suitable options, and I came across a new neighborhood in the county. Although we considered some other attractive offers, we decided that moving into a freshly built home would have its unique advantages.

We believed that moving into a new neighborhood would be a fresh start for our family. Being the first residents, we could experience the transition process and help the community grow. We were drawn to the idea of communal living, and we hoped to create lasting relationships with our neighbors. Furthermore, the neighborhood was situated in a prime location, which meant that we would have easy access to important amenities like schools, healthcare facilities, shopping centers, and public transportation. Additionally, the surrounding area was breathtakingly beautiful, with vast open spaces, parks, and lakes. We knew that this would be an ideal place to raise our children and spend time with our loved ones.

Also, since most of the facilities were new and had not been used by anyone before, we felt that this would allow us to design the interior according to our preferences. The decision to acquire a new home was a crucial one, and it took us considerable time to finalize it. Nonetheless, we were confident in our choice, and we relished the prospect of shaping our house exactly as we desired.

However, acquiring a new home was not without its challenges. One of the concerns we had was the expense of buying a new house. It was a significant investment, and we had to be mindful of our budget. We looked for ways to reduce costs, such as opting for basic amenities and adjusting our lifestyles accordingly. We also did extensive research and consultation before making any decisions. This ensured that we made informed choices and minimized the risks of complications down the road.

Nevertheless, the process of designing our new home was a thrilling experience. We had the freedom to create a space that reflected our personalities and preferences. We consulted with experts, such as interior designers, to help us make educated choices and also make changes to the house to suit our needs.

Looking back now on those decisive months in 2003 brings immense gratitude for the life Annie and I managed to create together. Through hard work and an unwavering belief in each other's abilities to overcome challenges, we turned a simple yearning for stability into our heartfelt reality.

One day, while sitting together with Anne and our children, we began discussing our thoughts about moving into a new home. My wife, always the pragmatic thinker, insisted that I meticulously evaluate our financial situation to determine the extent to which we could benefit from the program related to our desired housing arrangement. Mindful of her advice, I spent considerable time examining every aspect of our finances and weighing its implications on our future.

Upon completion of my analysis, I decided that it was a wise decision to invest in a newly developing housing scheme in the county. The construction of our dream apartment complex was still ongoing, which meant that we had to be patient for some time before reaping the benefits of our investment. The excitement grew within us as we anticipated finally moving into a place that we could call our own.

Time moved forward, and the construction progressed at a steady pace. Even though it required two long years for us to finally witness the completion of our new home, it was undoubtedly worth the wait. As each month passed by in those two years, we eagerly tracked the developments taking place at the construction site. Every brick laid and every wall painted was one step closer to realizing our dream.

The connection between each of these events enhanced our appreciation for the importance of meticulous planning and foresight in life as individuals and as a family. We learned that an investment in a stable and secure future goes beyond just monetary calculations; it also extends to nurturing strong relationships within the family unit and instilling the values essential to living a fulfilling life.

Indeed, March 2005 marked a milestone in our lives when we finally saw this dream materialize into reality. After patiently waiting for two years, experiencing countless discussions with Anne and the children about how we envisioned making this space truly ours—filled with love and laughter—we closed on the house and moved in at last.

As I reminisce about that wonderful day when we officially started living in this house, I am filled with immense gratitude for the journey that led us there. It has been a long and sometimes challenging road, but today we are stronger, wiser, and more appreciative of the life we have built together within these walls.

Over the years, our house has transformed not only in appearance but also in the memories it holds. Birthdays and holidays have come and gone, and our children have grown through each milestone within this space we call home. The laughter of our family sharing a meal at the dinner table echoes through the rooms while photographs adorning our walls capture moments we will cherish forever.

Our home is more than just a place to rest our heads at night; it is a living testament to our love, dedication, and commitment to providing the best possible future for ourselves and those who will inherit it one day.

In conclusion, moving into a new house was the right choice for our family. It offered us a chance to start fresh in a new community and build lasting relationships with our neighbors. The lessons learned from this experience continue to resonate even now as I happily reside here with Anne and our children. Our home serves as a constant reminder of the value of diligence in not only financial matters but also nurturing strong relationships—all crucial components of creating a lasting legacy. While all this was not without its challenges, the experience of designing and customizing our new home was exciting and rewarding. We were thrilled to be one of the first occupants in the neighborhood and were eager to see it grow.

Chapter 16
My Certification Path

After making the difficult decision to close my restaurant, I found myself contemplating various avenues before returning to work for someone else. One key aspect I wanted to focus on was establishing myself as a food service professional. To fully commit to this goal, I decided to give up both marijuana and alcohol, which had been part of my life for years. Concurrently, I aimed to advance my culinary education, building upon my skills and passion for the craft.

I am proud to share that with persistence and determination, I successfully quit using marijuana and alcohol. This significant personal achievement paved the way for me to pursue my ultimate dream of becoming a Certified Executive Chef (CEC). Additionally, earning this prestigious title held the promise of allowing me to join the esteemed American Culinary Federation (ACF), an organization that represents the highest standards in the industry.

Emboldened by a clear vision and unwavering determination, I embarked on a demanding journey with the American Culinary Federation. This path toward achieving CEC certification proved challenging and rewarding in equal measure; it was an extraordinary adventure spanning nearly five years. Throughout this enriching experience, I honed my culinary prowess while simultaneously fulfilling my deepest desire to excel in the competitive world of professional cooking.

To embark on the journey toward becoming a Certified Executive Chef (CEC), there are several crucial prerequisites one must fulfill. First and foremost, it's essential to possess the right qualifications, which entail a minimum of three years of experience in the role of an executive chef. Additionally, having managed a team of at least five employees in the past is a must. Personally, I surpassed these requirements by running my own restaurant for a remarkable eight years. Throughout that period, I often had the pleasure of overseeing and guiding more than twenty employees, honing my expertise and leadership skills in the process.

Secondly, it was essential for me to have completed a culinary education program, which needed to encompass at least 80 hours of comprehensive teaching and learning experiences. Several methods were available to accomplish this requirement. However, the mandatory courses I had to undertake to achieve the highly sought-after CEC designation could also satisfy this prerequisite. The intriguing and informative courses delved into topics such as supervisory management, nutrition, and many advanced techniques in both cooking and baking. Additionally, the well-rounded curriculum featured a few other captivating classes that contributed to an engaging and dynamic educational journey.

An alternative method of satisfying this requirement involved actively participating and securing victories in competitions approved by the ACF. Participants were duly rewarded with credit, and those who managed to earn winning medals received even more points. The medals were categorized into three levels of distinction: Silver, Bronze, and Gold. Naturally, the better the performance, the higher the number of points awarded.

Throughout my journey, I enthusiastically partook in numerous contests and, as a result, emerged victorious with eight bronze medals to my name. Encouraged by my success, I continued to challenge myself by entering even more competitions. In due time, I managed to achieve all the prerequisites set forth by the ACF for CEC certification in my steadfast pursuit of personal growth and excellence.

In March of 2005, I achieved a significant milestone in my culinary journey by obtaining the prestigious CEC (Certified Executive Chef) certification for the very first time. This accomplishment not only boosted my confidence but also instilled in me a keen sense of responsibility to maintain and upgrade my culinary expertise continually. The CEC certification necessitated that I recertify every five years, which entailed 80 hours of continued education every five years.

As time progressed, my zest for learning and honing my skills propelled me to attend a multitude of specialized courses and actively participate in numerous culinary competitions on both national and international platforms. Each event provided me with a valuable opportunity to interact with fellow professionals, exchange ideas, gain insights on the latest trends, and expand my personal network—all of which contributed to making me a better chef.

My diligent efforts and dedication to the culinary profession eventually culminated in being recognized as an ACF (American Culinary Federation) approved culinary evaluator. This esteemed position bestowed upon me the honor of serving as a judge for various exams undertaken by other aspiring chefs. Over an illustrious ten-year period, I had the privilege of evaluating the practical cooking skills of as many as 60 talented individuals; each evaluation helped me learn something new and appreciate the unique ways in which budding chefs approach their craft.

Presently, I am still an esteemed member of the American Culinary Federation, maintaining steady growth within this dynamic organization. My next recertification is scheduled for 2025—an event where I plan not only to reaffirm my commitment but also benchmark myself against industry standards while staying true to my passion for the culinary arts.

During those transformative years, I began to experience discomfort and pain in my right hip, making day-to-day life a little more challenging than usual. Back in the early stages of 2001, I received a diagnosis of Osteoarthritis. This essentially implied that the cartilage within my right hip joint had eroded significantly, necessitating major hip replacement surgery sooner rather than later.

The actual procedure was eventually carried out a few years later, in April of 2009, during a particularly tumultuous time for the country as we faced a severe recession. I remember vividly how the mounting economic pressures weighed on me. Incredibly, just two days before my scheduled surgery, my employer was forced to lay me off due to economic difficulties. Talk about timing!

However, amid those bleak circumstances, hope shone through as the company I had been working for graciously agreed to cover my health insurance for an additional 18 months. Consequently, this helped ease some of the financial burdens I could otherwise have faced during such a critical time in my life.

So, most of the medical bills associated with the hip replacement surgery were taken care of by my insurance provider, much to my relief and gratitude. Reflecting on this experience, I can't help but feel thankful for that small silver lining during a period that's etched in my memory as both physically and emotionally challenging.

Following my surgery, I embarked on a journey of recovery that spanned over several months. The initial postoperative stage required dedicated care and attention to my back, with the first two weeks being particularly crucial. As my strength slowly returned, I began participating in tailored rehabilitation sessions led by an experienced physiotherapist who came to my aid three times a week.

These sessions formed the backbone of my recovery plan and helped to speed up my healing process. With each new session, I felt more secure in regaining my mobility and independence. To further support my progress, I was provided with a walker that greatly assisted in boosting my confidence during this transitional period.

As the weeks went by, it became evident that the rehabilitation was having a positive impact on my overall well-being. Not only was I physically recovering, but my energy levels blossomed as well. The once seemingly insurmountable challenge transformed into a rewarding and eye-opening experience that allowed me to truly appreciate the power of perseverance.

By the end of three months, I found myself back on solid ground—my feet steady and ready for whatever awaited me. The enthusiasm to return to work was tangible as I eagerly looked forward to resuming a sense of normalcy and continuing where I had left off before the surgery.

In retrospect, this harrowing yet ultimately transformative experience taught me invaluable lessons about determination and resilience—qualities I carry with me as permanent reminders of how far I've come and what truly lies within us all when faced with adversity.

Chapter 17
Working at the Vail Valley Medical Center

For the next three months, I found myself fully engrossed in searching for my next job. With a determined spirit, I explored every local opportunity that seemed like a good fit for my skills and interests. As time flew by, I began to worry if I would ever find something that aligned with my goals. Just when doubts started clouding my mind and when I least expected it, I received an exciting phone call.

The call was from an employer who had carefully reviewed my application and was eager to offer me a position at a prestigious hospital called Vail Valley Medical Center. The moment was bittersweet; although I was ecstatic about the new job, I knew that there was still one more hurdle to overcome before the position could be mine—the interview.

With a mix of anxiety and anticipation, I prepared diligently for the interview. Every evening after submitting applications, I researched the hospital's history, mission, and values, ensuring that I would be well-informed and confident when speaking with my potential employer. As luck would have it, my thorough preparation paid off as I impressed my interviewer with thoughtful answers and engaging conversation.

The experience at Vail Valley Medical Center enabled me to gain valuable insights into what truly matters in job searching—perseverance and self-belief. This challenging quest ultimately led me to appreciate not only the opportunities on my path but also the journey itself.

Shortly after joining the hospital, I received some news about their food service program and immediately learned that it would no longer be operated by the hospital itself. Instead, the reins were handed over to a renowned subsidiary company called Sodexo. This French-based giant was making waves as the largest company in the world within the food service management industry.

My excitement grew even more when I was hired as the New Executive Chef at the hospital while joining hands with a multinational company. I could feel that my culinary journey was taking an incredible turn, but little did I know my first steps would lead me to a new adventure in Washington State.

Embarking on the new journey, I ended up in Everett, a picturesque town just 25 miles north of Seattle, where my two-week Sodexo training period began. The state-of-the-art facility welcomed me as I dove headfirst into learning the ins and outs of all the relevant operations in the prestigious company. Throughout my time at the training center, I studied not only Sodexo's unique tools and equipment but also its menus, mouthwatering recipes, corporate protocols, and standards for excellence. The experience proved to be enlightening as I listened attentively to seasoned facilitators eager to share their wealth of knowledge.

As my training drew to a close, I was filled with anticipation for what lay ahead: returning to Vail Valley Medical Center as an integral part of the management team. It was clear that this opportunity would not only strengthen my skills as an executive chef but also deepen my connection to such an innovative and forward-thinking industry leader.

So, now, fully equipped with newfound expertise and enthusiasm, I was more than eager to embark on this extraordinary culinary journey alongside Sodexo and revolutionize Vail Valley Medical Center's food service program.

During my first year at work, I noticed the opportunity to enhance the partnership between Sodexo and the hospital. This led to the realization that the present computer system at the hospital needed to be overhauled. To ensure the continued partnership, I maintained the use of the current system until we gradually transitioned to the Sodexo platform. This meant that the kitchen had a dual-functional system to cater to employees and patients, but the transition was crucial in providing patients with healthier food options.

As the hospital only accommodated 50 patients at most, naturally, a significant part of the menu was designed for the 300 employees. I took up this challenge with much openness and familiarity since I had prior experience in preparing large-scale food productions from working in hotels, where I had run food operations in the banquet department. I thought I was doing a good job when I got to know that the hospital employees were happy with the menu changes and almost always appreciated the meals we served them. Needless to say, this made me happy.

Within the span of a year, we finally completed the renovation and shifted to the new Sodexo system. This new system had its advantages as it standardized the entire menu leading to less experimentation and room for novelty. This meant I no longer had to work as hard as I did when I accepted the job. While it was relieving initially, I soon became bored with it and felt that it limited my creative freedom, causing me to enjoy my job less. However, I didn't allow room for complacency and persevered and continued working for the hospital for 18 long months.

Then, one day, I was summoned to meet with my supervisor, who informed me that my team had raised concerns about my management style. Initially, I was given a written warning, which quickly escalated to severe issues. I was taken aback as I always treated my staff with the utmost respect and professionalism and never had any issues with them in the past. I felt this was more of a political move than anything else. Thus, I refused to give in.

As time progressed, it became clear that the hospital management wanted me out, and they were actively trying to push me to resign. Nevertheless, I refused to back down, standing my ground unwaveringly. Ultimately, the only way for me to leave was for them to fire me.

On another occasion, while I was busy working in the kitchen, preparing the food, I faced an unexpected challenge when one of my subordinates refused to follow my directions. Although I was patient and polite in requesting his cooperation to complete the tasks that were assigned to him, he chose to throw a tantrum instead. Unfortunately, this dramatic outburst occurred right in front of my boss, which led to unfounded accusations of improper employee management against me.

As a result of this incident, I was unfairly terminated from my position. The irony is that just two weeks after my dismissal, the very employee who made a fuss and complained against me was fired for coming to work intoxicated. I wasn't surprised at all.

Looking back, I believe that I had been a valuable asset to the hospital food service program and that my termination was unjust. Being caught up in the whirlwind of office politics, I found myself out of work once again.

However, I remained hopeful for a brighter future. With each day presenting new opportunities, I resolved to move forward and pursue better things that life had to offer. It was an important lesson and a reminder that sometimes the most challenging situations can become sources of strength and motivation for future success.

Chapter 18
A Time for Reflection

Life may not always be fair, and it certainly won't always be easy or without challenges. However, it will consistently present a multitude of new opportunities for growth and discovery, particularly when you steadfastly refuse to give up in the pursuit of your passions. The saying goes that winners never quit, while quitters never win; this life lesson is something I gleaned from my father many years ago during his time as a successful businessman.

In the factory that he owned, the primary products manufactured were cash registers and machine papers. He not only managed his responsibilities with due diligence but also forged strong partnerships with others in his field. Being fully aware of the chilly conditions in the warehouse where his employees worked, my dad and his partners provided the workers with warm shirts that featured inspiring quotes printed on them. Some examples of these motivational maxims include "Plan your work and work your plan" and "When the going gets tough, the tough get going."

These words of wisdom have resonated with me throughout my life. Whenever I find myself reflecting on those early days in my father's factory, it serves as a source of motivation to push with even greater determination toward achieving my goals. It's a constant reminder of how perseverance in the face of adversity can lead to real success over time, transforming challenges into triumphs and setbacks into stepping stones on the path to fulfilling one's dreams.

I spent some time reflecting on this specific period of my life, primarily because I felt somewhat down and disheartened after losing my once stable job at the renowned hospital in Vail. This sudden loss affected me deeply, and in an attempt to seek justice, I tried to file a formal complaint with the Equal Employment Opportunity Commission (EEOC). However, much to my dismay, the staff at the EEOC displayed an uncooperative attitude and were unwilling to provide any substantial assistance.

As time passed, I eventually realized that I had already lost enough precious sleep fretting over this unfortunate situation. Thus, I finally decided to put all these setbacks and negative emotions behind me. Instead of dwelling on the past, I focused on my true passion—cooking. With unshakable resolve, I pursued a fulfilling career as a professional chef and dedicated myself wholeheartedly to perfecting my culinary skills.

Additionally, during these challenging months, I experienced profound sorrow when my cherished father passed away unexpectedly. He became gravely ill, and ultimately, I lost him to the cruel hands of death. The pain and emotional turmoil of watching him leave this world was overwhelming, especially considering he had always been my biggest inspiration in life. With his absence, I needed to find a sense of peace and come to terms with this devastating loss. As a result, I decided to take a break from everything and retreat into the sanctuary of my home for a much-needed period of mourning.

This temporary hiatus in my professional journey also provided me with an invaluable opportunity for reflection and personal growth. Coincidentally, it was during the 2000s, the early days of the World Wide Web, when the internet was experiencing an unprecedented boom. At that time, I had yet to fully comprehend how the World Wide Web and social media were revolutionizing our global landscape. Intrigued by the possibilities, I purchased a cutting-edge Apple laptop, which helped reignite some of my long-lost passions.

Throughout my entire life, playing the guitar has been a cherished hobby that brought me tremendous joy. As fate would have it, while browsing through various websites one day, I stumbled across an innovative digital platform that offered guitar lessons online. These virtual classes proved to be a welcome distraction as I navigated the laborious process of finding new employment.

Alongside this newfound interest, I made another unexpected discovery in the form of a celebrated book reviewer by the name of Tai Lopez. Enthralled by his recommendations, I immersed myself in several thought-provoking books he suggested as essential reading material.

My explorations also led me into the realm of affiliate marketing—a potential business endeavor where I identified a unique opportunity to generate additional income on top of my regular salary. Eager to delve deeper into this intriguing concept, I found myself held back by Anne's reluctance over such pursuits. Respecting her apprehensions, I eventually chose to abandon this venture for the time being.

After giving it some thought, I decided to enroll in the esteemed School of Culinary Arts, which was located in the picturesque city of Boulder, Colorado. The school operated on a strict schedule, with classes taking place from early 7 a.m. until 3 p.m. each day. Unfortunately, the school's location proved to be somewhat inconvenient for me since my house was three hours away, making commuting a challenge.

With classes scheduled from Monday through Friday every week, I knew that I needed to come up with a more reasonable solution for getting to and from school. As a result, I began considering the possibility of finding a temporary apartment to rent near the school's premises.

Anne, my partner, initially seemed less than enthusiastic about the idea of me relocating and living apart from her for an extended period. However, after several discussions and in-depth deliberations, we ultimately came to a mutual agreement that this move was in my best interest academically. With our shared understanding in place, I started searching for an apartment close to the school to reduce my daily travel time and allow me to focus more on my culinary education.

Fortunately, almost in a stroke of luck, I managed to discover an available apartment situated just across the street from the school I wanted to attend. With my living situation sorted out, my next challenge was to secure funding to finance both my education and my stay in the beautiful city of Boulder. To help me achieve this goal, the school administration kindly assisted me by setting up a convenient loan system. This solution worked perfectly for me, allowing me to start my fascinating journey at the prestigious culinary institute.

Over the next six months, I would diligently leave my home at 4 a.m. every Monday to make it in time for class. I would then dedicate the rest of my weekdays to studying and immersing myself in all that Boulder had to offer. However, on Friday afternoons, I made it a point to return home to spend some quality time with my beloved family over the weekends.

Despite being physically apart during the weekdays, maintaining constant communication with Anne was incredibly important. We would regularly engage in lengthy phone calls discussing our lives and planning delightful family retreats on weekends.

One of our absolute favorite activities was spending warm evenings at Red Rock Amphitheater in Morrison, Colorado. The serene atmosphere was idyllic as we would delightfully lose ourselves in listening to live music from various remarkable bands near and dear to our hearts. On particularly special occasions, we were fortunate enough to witness awe-inspiring performances from legendary bands like Tom Petty and The Heartbreakers, Widespread Panic, and magnificent Renditions of The Grateful Dead, among many other incredibly talented musicians who captivated us with their enthralling tunes amid an electrifying live audience.

Once the weekends ended, I found myself returning to Boulder. It wasn't a decision that came easily to me, but it was one that I felt had to be made to progress further. My primary goal was to refine my skills as a chef, and Chef Dan proved to be an exceptional mentor in this journey. He possessed an extensive repertoire of knowledge that would prove to be invaluable in the forthcoming years of my culinary career.

Dan himself had accumulated twenty years of rich cooking experience within the industry. He generously shared every bit of his wisdom and insight with his students, ensuring we were equipped with the tools needed for success. Eager to learn from such a seasoned professional, I paid close attention throughout his lessons and eagerly absorbed every piece of information he offered, much like a sponge soaking up water.

Through these immersive lessons, I significantly enhanced my understanding of bread production and working with chocolate to produce an assortment of exquisite pastries. In addition, I acquired the skills necessary for creating various chocolate showpieces and artistically plated desserts. Our curriculum also encompassed gluten-free and vegan baking techniques, broadening my baking capabilities even further.

During my time at the institute, I attended every class without fail and consistently participated in all activities presented by Chef Dan. After completing the rigorous course, I felt immensely gratified by all the effort I had put forth. Upon completing the course, my hard work was rewarded with a high B average, which left me feeling deeply satisfied and proud of my accomplishments.

Another motivating factor for enrolling in this course was its potential to contribute toward my ACF recertification, due in 2015. The final requirement for completing this program was undertaking an externship. For this endeavor, I chose Westin −conveniently close to my residence in Avon, Colorado.

My externship allowed me the privilege of working closely with Chef Jonathon. Under his guidance, we participated in the prestigious Beaver Creek Ginger Bread House Competition, securing an impressive second-place finish. The competition was fierce, and I could not be prouder of our achievement in this respected event.

As my time with the culinary school ended, I found myself eagerly anticipating the next chapter of my life. I decided that finding a satisfying job would be my primary objective. This search led me to discover an enticing opportunity at Vail Resorts, where I was offered a position working on the mountain within the exclusive Game Creek Club.

My role at the club was that of an Assistant Pastry Chef, and I had the privilege to work alongside the esteemed Chef Dave. Under his expert guidance, I honed my skills and learned the nuances of crafting elegant and delicious pastries. The primary responsibility of my role was to design, create, and maintain an impressive dessert buffet meant to entice and delight our esteemed guests.

This mouthwatering spread featured a diverse selection of confectionary delights ranging from exquisitely layered cakes and silky-smooth custards to dainty Petit fours, crumbly cookies, and artisanal chocolates. Each day presented a fresh challenge to excel in the art of patisserie while ensuring that our discerning clientele was always left wanting more.

One of the greatest perks of working at Vail Resorts was indulging in my passion for skiing. The resort was situated on Mountain Vail, affording me countless opportunities to hit the slopes during my tenure there. As such, I was able to merge both my professional ambitions as a chef with my love for outdoor activities in this picturesque mountain setting.

I spent two memorable years in this role, from 2012 until 2014. During this time, not only did I have the pleasure of developing as a culinary artist and avid skier but also fostering meaningful relationships with colleagues who shared my interests and pursuits.

During this period of my life, I also had the opportunity to work at a popular local Japanese restaurant situated in Edwards. My role involved working at the wok station as a part-time employee, primarily during winter. This experience turned out to be quite enjoyable as I had the chance to earn some additional income during that particular season. However, as the ski season eventually ended, I found myself searching for alternative employment opportunities.

An extraordinary opportunity presented itself when the USA Culinary Olympic team descended upon Denver to conduct tryouts for their esteemed squad. Despite being a student at the time, I was granted the remarkable privilege of serving as an assistant to the competing chefs. This role placed me alongside the coaching team, offering my assistance in food presentations and supporting the participants vying for coveted spots on the USA Culinary Olympic team.

Witnessing the intense competition, the creativity, and the meticulous craftsmanship involved in the culinary realm was nothing short of awe-inspiring. From the moment the chefs began conceptualizing their dishes to the final presentation, I was intricately involved in their journey. It was a truly remarkable experience to contribute to the endeavors of these accomplished chefs who aspired to represent the United States on the grand stage of the Culinary Olympics.

The dedication and skill of the ACF culinary team USA were abundantly evident, culminating in their triumphant third-place finish at the prestigious Villeroy and Boch Culinary World Cup held in Luxembourg in 2014. The team's exceptional performance earned them two gold medals and the highest score in a cold food competition. The competitors showcased their culinary prowess through an array of stunning creations, including elaborate buffet platters featuring seafood, meat, and game, as well as a sumptuous four-course dinner and tantalizing finger foods.

This opportunity to work alongside the culinary Olympians was an experience that left an indelible mark on my culinary journey, deepening my appreciation for the artistry, precision, and innovation that elevate the culinary world to new heights.

During my time at the prestigious baking school, I had not only acquired a wide range of new skills but also managed to refine and harness some of my prior expertise. This entire experience played a significant role in helping me grow and evolve into a more accomplished chef. Since I had only recently wrapped up my comprehensive baking lessons, it seemed like the perfect time to start searching for a job that would allow me to put my newfound abilities to good use.

As luck would have it, an exceptional artisan bread bakery called Avon Bakery was situated not too far from where I lived. Upon applying, they were more than happy to offer me a position and even placed me in charge of bread production, which was quite an exciting prospect for me. The only catch was that my work shift started at 9 p.m. and continued until 4 a.m., which was quite challenging initially.

Truth be told, both my wife Anne and I found the unusual schedule rather difficult to adapt to at first. However, after some discussion and careful consideration, we both eventually came to the agreement that I should indeed accept the job offer. Over time, I found myself acclimating quite well to the peculiar working hours and soon began thriving in my new position.

An unexpected bonus of being employed on a night shift was that it awarded me ample free time during the early evenings. As an avid guitar player, this development was particularly delightful as it granted me ample opportunities to play guitar and indulge in one of my deeply cherished passions. The additional leisure time spent doing something I truly enjoyed served as a wonderful source of relaxation, ultimately contributing to a heightened sense of happiness and overall satisfaction with life.

As soon as I commenced working at the bakery, it quickly became apparent that my list of responsibilities would grow steadily more extensive. Tasked with scaling, shaping, proofing, and baking the bread itself, I found myself accountable for overseeing the entire process. Producing bread on such a large scale was no easy feat, and it required a great deal of arduous and painstaking work. Nevertheless, I wholeheartedly embraced the challenge and discovered that, much to my surprise, I genuinely enjoyed every minute of it.

During those particular months, I started experiencing pain in my left hip from time to time. Gradually, the pain became more intense and unbearable, which negatively impacted my ability to carry out my job responsibilities effectively. It was at this moment that I came to the conclusion that the issue with my hip was far more severe than I had initially thought. As my overall health continued to deteriorate, I found myself unable to continue working at the bakery any longer.

Consequently, I made the decision to resign from my position and started making preparations for undergoing another hip replacement surgery.

Thankfully, the surgical procedure was successful and went smoothly. Afterward, the medical professionals attending to me recommended that I set aside a significant amount of rest and recovery to properly heal. After that, I was discharged and allowed to return home on the same day. Once there, I focused on getting ample rest while being surrounded by the love and support of my family members. In particular, I will always be eternally grateful to my wife for providing me with unwavering encouragement and assistance throughout the recovery process.

The recovery process, after the challenging and transformative experience I went through, took almost four long, contemplative months. During this time of introspection, I found myself reflecting on the many twists and turns of my unique career trajectory. I started devising a solid plan for the next steps that would inevitably shape the future direction I wanted to head in.

As I pondered throughout my incredibly rigorous journey – with all its highs, lows, and memorable moments – I slowly but surely concluded that perhaps the most optimal way forward for me would involve delving back into the world of dessert preparation. This realm had always sparked my interest, passion, and a strong sense of fulfillment when crafting these delectable treats for others to enjoy.

With renewed determination, I began an extensive search for a job opportunity that would align with my skills, personal goals, and values. After much effort, I finally found a suitable position at a highly-regarded establishment called Vista Restaurant in the charming town of Edwards.

Accepting the job offer at Vista Restaurant was an easy decision for me. Not only was it conveniently located close to my home, which was an added bonus, but it also provided me with ample freedom to express my creativity while working on their impressive dessert menu—a task that made me truly excited about what lay ahead.

Another reason why Vista Restaurant felt like the perfect fit was due to its talented and esteemed head chef, Chef Dave. Not only was he an incredible mentor who constantly supported and encouraged me to expand my culinary horizons, but his immense knowledge about desserts allowed me to delve deeper into this fascinating world and learn even more tips, tricks, and techniques that honed my skills as an expert dessert chef.

Chapter 19
From Pastries to Presidents

During the early winter months of 2016, a life-altering incident occurred—my mother suffered a terrible fall. She ended up having a broken hip and had to be immediately hospitalized for proper medical attention. This unforeseen situation forced me to take a break from my professional life and return home to assist my siblings and take care of our ailing mother. As a result, I had no choice but to submit my resignation from my cherished job at the restaurant, consequently putting my career on hold for several months.

As I devoted my time to caring for my mother at home, I couldn't help but notice her steadily deteriorating health. Her once lively spirit was slowly succumbing to her physical fragility, and it was heartbreaking to witness. Over time, her weakened condition led to her untimely demise— a moment that left me utterly devastated and distressed. Losing the remarkable woman who had been a constant source of inspiration throughout my journey was an earth-shattering event; she was the primary catalyst behind my pursuit of becoming a chef.

To make matters worse, I had already lost my father just a couple of years before this tragedy. The burden of losing both parents weighed heavily upon my soul. To this day, their memories remain ever-present in my heart, and I fondly reminisce about the cherished times we spent together.

After allowing myself some weeks to grieve and regroup, I decided that it was time to move forward and resume my professional endeavors. With resolved determination, I returned to Vista in hopes of reintegrating myself into the restaurant business. However, Vista was a seasonal restaurant that typically closed its doors for six weeks during the transitional period between the summer and winter seasons. Consequently, circumstances called for me to seek out alternative employment opportunities elsewhere—yet I had no idea where fate would ultimately lead me on this unpredictable journey.

Fortunately, a refreshingly themed restaurant situated at a golf course close to my hometown had recently opened its doors. The establishment was owned by the renowned Kelly Liken Harvest and managed under the umbrella of the esteemed Sonnenalp Hotel. In a previous endeavor, I had the privilege of working alongside Kelly at Rick and Kellie's, located in Edwards. Rick, Kelly's husband, jointly operated the restaurant together with Chef Julian. My main responsibility in that role was in the pastry department and primarily focused on the creation of delicious desserts.

Kelly also had another restaurant located within the charming town of Vail. She bravely chose to showcase her culinary prowess on Iron Chef America, where she narrowly missed out on victory against Chef Jose Garces. Following this experience, she closed her Vail establishment and collaborated with Sonnenalp Hotel to bring forth Harvest at the Single Tree Golf Course, which was owned by the hotel.

One unexpected winter season, Kelly encountered Anne while dining at Anne's workplace. In a casual conversation, Anne asked if there were any opportunities available at Harvest. As if perfectly orchestrated by destiny itself, Kelly mentioned her pastry chef, who had just put in their resignation. During their exchange, Anne recommended that I meet with Kelly, an offer I eagerly took.

Following a brief interview with Kelly, I was ecstatic to accept the position of Pastry Chef. An invigorating new challenge lay before me. Working there was thoroughly enjoyable but quite unexpectedly, Kelly departed from the restaurant merely a couple of months after I joined. Subsequently, I pursued internal promotion for her vacated role but was unsuccessful; eventually, Chef Rosa filled her shoes while I continued as Pastry Chef.

One particularly enjoyable aspect of my role was the creative liberty I held to craft dishes for our menu and select desired recipes based on my preferences. Traditional favorites I often chose included the sumptuous flourless chocolate cake accompanied by hand-crafted pistachio ice cream. Additionally, my culinary repertoire featured a variety of delectable ice creams and iconic items such as Apple strudel and the classic crème Brulé.

My absolute favorite creation was an oversized blueberry muffin laden with streusel topping, alongside a uniquely flavorful Morning Glory muffin comprised of grated apple and carrot. Beyond pastries, I cultivated an extensive list of fresh smoothies, invigorating sorbets, and an array of eclectic ice creams that were meticulously prepared every day.

One of the most exhilarating aspects of my job was handling the pastry and bread creation for various events hosted by the restaurant. These events frequently included weddings, club gatherings, and exclusive parties. My responsibilities involved crafting a variety of cakes, bread, and authentic French-style pastries.

During my time at the restaurant, a female club member arrived one day to announce that a renowned former White House chef would be orchestrating a wine dinner. When I found out it was John Moeller, it rang a bell. I had encountered this name before but couldn't quite put my finger on it. Excited and curious, I eagerly anticipated his arrival, hoping that seeing his face might jog my memory.

On June 14th, John finally arrived to begin preparations for the wine dinner. Upon meeting him, we engaged in a brief conversation, discussing his professional history and how he ultimately found himself working at the White House. We promptly began our respective tasks for the day's dinner event. Though I primarily focused on my menu, Chef Moeller requested that I create several dessert items of his liking.

Despite our interaction earlier in the day, I still couldn't recall where I had previously encountered John. With this mystery on my mind, I returned home and spent the evening deep in thought until suddenly, it clicked – back in 1988! At that time, I was employed at the Westin in Vail when I received an invitation to visit their sister's property in Washington, DC. There, I enjoyed a two-month stay as they graciously accommodated me. Much to my surprise, one of the chefs working in the fine-dining restaurant at this hotel was none other than John Moeller himself.

Recalling our time together now brought a flood of memories – John was not only an outstanding chef but also an amazing person. He even took me to his parents' house during our time together. This had been nearly three decades ago, and when I finally shared this revelation with John, he, too, remembered our earlier interaction in DC. I was delighted to reconnect with him after all these years, and as fate would have it, our encounter took place just a year and a half before he accepted the prestigious position at the White House.

In addition to his various accomplishments, John proudly promoted his recently released book titled *Dining at the White House.* Having purchased a copy for myself, I had the honor of receiving his autograph and even captured a memorable photograph with him during our time working together. As I delved into the pages of his book, my admiration for this man grew exponentially. The captivating stories within truly resonated with me, and for those who find enjoyment in reading about the intriguing lives of chefs, I wholeheartedly encourage you to explore John's literary work. Furthermore, it's worth noting that John owns and operates both a restaurant and a catering business in the charming town of Lancaster, Pennsylvania.

After reading John's book, I could relate to his story. Pursuing a career as a chef can prove to be quite demanding, yet it offers the unique opportunity to encounter individuals originating from diverse walks of life. These fascinating encounters often result in the creation of cherished memories that remain etched in our minds for years to come.

Chapter 20
Eat Well – Live Well

Even though managing the restaurant proved to be quite laborious, its operations were merely seasonal, which effectively left me with a relatively lighter workload during the spring and fall seasons. Consequently, in 2018, when I found myself with an abundance of free time, I opted to take up employment as an Uber driver to supplement my income.

The entire experience turned out to be genuinely rewarding as it not only allowed me to substantially boost my earnings but also provided me with ample flexibility since I essentially operated my own rideshare business. I was at liberty to activate the app whenever it suited my schedule and didn't feel compelled to work if fatigue set in. One of the most fascinating aspects of this endeavor was undoubtedly the array of unique individuals I had the pleasure of encountering and assisting with their transportation requirements.

In January 2020, I received a request from the executive committee of the hotel situated in the picturesque Vail. They needed an individual possessing my unique skill set and experience to oversee guest services at an alternate location. The restaurant was owned by the same company but was at the renowned Sonnenalp Hotel. Basically, it involved me moving from one part of the company to another.

There, my assignment was to collaborate with Chef Julian, an exceptionally talented professional in his field. We immediately developed a strong rapport and enjoyed working together. However, the most challenging aspect of this role was coping with the outdated kitchens not originally designed to accommodate the increased volume of business that the hotel had experienced over time.

On a more positive note, an ambitious plan was underway to invest six million dollars in revamping the facilities, ensuring the kitchens would effectively cater to their growing clientele. This intrigued me, as I fully supported the visionary approach envisaged by the hotel's management. As a result, I decided to stay with the establishment throughout this extensive renovation project.

Unfortunately, before any progress could be made on these improvements, the world was blindsided by the COVID-19 pandemic. This extraordinary event left an indelible impact on everyone's lives around the globe.

The entire country experienced a lockdown, which brought about an adverse impact on all business sectors. Our hotel wasn't exempt from the ordeal, subsequently forcing us to close our doors for three months. Our hotel's revered Chef, who initially hailed from Germany, faced the unfortunate consequence of the pandemic, compelling him to return to his homeland during this period. Despite these grim circumstances that encompassed everyone, it unexpectedly turned out to be a silver lining for me.

While most regions within the country remained closed for an extended duration, the county of Vail emerged as an exception by reopening much sooner. After being entirely closed in March 2021, we recommenced operations by June 2021. As a result, Vail became one of the few destinations where people could visit and experience some sense of normalcy. Correspondingly, with the resumption of activities came a comprehensive list of protocols that were obligatory for everyone to follow. Adhering to these stringent guidelines posed a significant challenge for us to ensure our business persevered while simultaneously safeguarding the well-being of all involved parties.

By that point, the hotel had appointed a new Executive Chef scheduled to commence his role in July of that year. The talented chef had amassed five years of experience working in Asia and had decided to return to his home country due to the COVID-19 pandemic. Eagerly anticipating the upcoming refurbishment, we joined forces and worked together seamlessly.

However, the renovation process wasn't set to conclude until Autumn 2022. Both Chef Josh and I found working amid the renovations rather challenging. There were instances when we needed to close off the cafeteria area and relocate operations to a significantly larger ballroom. This was primarily due to rigorous safety protocols implemented due to COVID-19. During this period, only cold food items were available for employees, consisting of an assortment of sandwiches and a modest selection of salads.

As the renovation project drew closer to completion, COVID-related restrictions gradually began to ease. Consequently, Chef Josh and I resumed utilizing the kitchen facilities for food preparation. By this juncture, we had established a strong working relationship built on mutual respect and appreciation for each other's skills. Over time, my admiration for Chef Josh continued to grow, and he became the best colleague I had ever had the pleasure to collaborate with throughout my entire professional journey.

The entire experience was genuinely enriching and rewarding for me. I consider myself incredibly fortunate to work alongside such an exceptional individual. Moreover, it is worth acknowledging the hotel owners' exceptional support in providing us with the optimal work environment – easily one of the most outstanding contexts I have ever encountered.

Despite its challenges, being a chef is no easy feat. The nature of the job is constantly bustling, demanding long work hours. Throughout my entire career, I have often found myself working on weekends and even during holidays. Sometimes, the exhaustion can catch up to you, making it imperative for chefs to maintain their physical fitness. Not only does it involve standing on your feet for extended periods, but it also calls for self-motivation and commendable organizational skills within the kitchen. Additionally, one must possess an intuitive sense of catering to food orders and mastery over both basic and advanced cooking and baking techniques.

One of the most substantial challenges in the culinary industry lies in learning to work with various individuals who become part of your team. Managing and collaborating with so many different people can be tough, and it is only through pure passion and a profound drive that a person can thrive in this field over a lengthy time.

As I continue on my career path, I am energized by the unique challenges faced by everyone within the industry. I frequently ponder whether other chefs of my age group are capable of adapting to changes triggered by technology's entrance into our profession.

The impact of the internet on the culinary world has always intrigued me. So much so that I have set a new goal: to establish an online business focused on imparting my decades-worth of skill and knowledge to others. While this venture is still in development, once it's up and running, I hope you'll join me on this exciting journey.

For those interested, you can find me on Facebook under the name PeterCBrenne CEC and in a Facebook group titled "Food and Cooking: A Pathway to Becoming a Chef." You can also catch me on YouTube under the channel Modern Food Concepts.

My motto? Eat Well – Live Well.

Section 2
Welcome To the World of Cooking

Introduction

By now, you're probably familiar with my story. I've been in the food service industry for over four decades, working in professional kitchens. I started out by learning and following recipes to the letter. This strict adherence to standards ensures consistency in the final product, which is a common practice in most restaurants and food establishments. And that's where my culinary journey began.

As my career progressed, I found myself in the hotel industry, creating recipes for various outlets like restaurants, banquet events, and quick service settings.

Currently, I'm employed at the Sonnenalp Hotel in Vail, Colorado, where I'm responsible for crafting meals for our employee cafeteria. Every year, I whip up thousands of meals, many of which feature my own personally developed recipes.

Through experience, I've learned the more you invest in the culinary world, the more you appreciate the immense knowledge required to master this exquisite art.

I believe cooking is a beautiful fusion of science and art, where the molecular structure of food is skillfully altered to enhance its taste. For me, the true essence of cooking lies in the artful combination of scientific principles and the pairing of ingredients, taking a simple meal to new heights of enjoyment.

In this section of the book, I want to share with you some of the recipes I've perfected over the years. My aim is to provide you with exciting and thought-provoking ideas that will help you gain the knowledge and skills needed to create extraordinary dishes for yourself. Remember, menus and recipes are just tools that guide us toward making fresh and nutritious meals, ultimately improving our overall well-being.

In the realm of Western culture, we have become familiar with the concept of menus. Generally, menus can be divided into seven categories, each serving a specific purpose:

1. Hors d'oeuvre - These are like little party favors that kick off the meal. Some can be enjoyed separately or as a prelude to the main course.

2. Soups - A warm and comforting start to any meal.

3. Appetizers - Small bites that tease the taste buds and get us excited for what's to come.

4. Salads - A refreshing and healthy option to cleanse the palate before the main event.

5. Main Course - The star of the show, where the real magic happens. This is where we indulge in our favorite dishes.

6. Dessert - The sweet finale that satisfies our cravings and leaves us with a smile on our faces.

7. Mignardise - The grand finale of a splendid meal. These delightful treats are enjoyed alongside a cup of coffee or a post-dinner cocktail.

In the following pages, I will present a wide range of recipes that will be a part of each one of the above-mentioned categories, from mouthwatering baked goods to tantalizing soups, refreshing salads and dressings, enticing appetizers, succulent fish and seafood courses, delightful vegetable dishes, satisfying entrees, and even some irresistible desserts. There is something for everyone!

I encourage you to have fun with these recipes because cooking should be a delightful and creative process. Our basic approach to menus can be divided into breakfast, lunch, and dinner. In this section of the book, we will explore the later part that can be divided.

Note: Please note that ingredient availability may vary depending on where you are in the world, and the limitations of your kitchen and equipment should also be considered. However, rest assured that there are often alternative ways to achieve similar results, and I will provide options in the recipes when applicable. My hope is that these ideas will bring you immense joy and satisfaction in your culinary adventures.

Cranberry Scone

Note:

Scones can be made using a two-part recipe. First, you will create the dry mix, which can be stored in an air-tight container in a cool, dry place. This recipe includes dry cranberries as the fruit component, but feel free to substitute fresh or dry fruits of your choice. You can also experiment with savory options like bacon and onions. Adjustments may need to be made for high-altitude baking, such as reducing the amount of chemical leavening used. For sea level, use three teaspoons of leavening. Additionally, to achieve a crispy exterior, start with higher heat for 10 minutes and then lower the temperature for the remaining cooking time.

To make the Dry Mix, you will need the following:

- 1 pound + 2 ounces all-purpose flour

- ¼ pound granulated sugar

- 1 ½ teaspoons salt

- 1 ½ teaspoons baking powder

To make the Scones, you will need the following:

- 1 ¼ cups dry scone mix

- ¼ cup buttermilk

- ¼ cup cold cubed butter

- 1 small egg, about 2oz

- 1 tsp vanilla extract

- Zest from 1/4 of an orange

- 2 tbsp orange juice

- ¼ cup dry cranberries

Here's the step-by-step procedure:

- In a bowl, combine the dry ingredients from the dry mix recipe.

- In a separate bowl, mix together buttermilk, eggs, vanilla extract, orange zest, and orange juice.

- Combine the wet and dry ingredients, mixing until just combined.

- Fold in the cold, cubed butter.

- Add the dry cranberries and gently fold them into the dough.

- Preheat the oven to 370 degrees Fahrenheit.

- Scoop the dough onto a baking sheet and shape it into scones.

- Bake for approximately 20 minutes or until the internal temperature reaches 200 degrees Fahrenheit.

Oatmeal Raisin Cookies

Note:

Oat meal raisin cookies are one of my all-time favorites. Like many people, I enjoy them when they are chewy. To achieve a chewy consistency, I use a combination of butter and organic shortening in baking at about 8000 feet above sea level. Cookies usually use a chemical levering agent such as baking soda or baking powder at this altitude, I cut those ingredients in half. If you are at sea level, you will double the amount of baking powder and baking soda in this recipe.

After some experimentation, I found that using half the number of raisins and substituting dry cranberries yields a delicious result. Then I will top the cookies with chopped walnuts and pecans

To make the Oatmeal Raisin Cookies, you will need the following:

- ¼ cup s butter

- ¼ cup organic palm shortening

- ¾ cups brown sugar

- ½ cup granulated sugar

- 2 eggs

- 1 tsp vanilla extract

- 1 ½ cups AP flour

- 3 cups quick-cooking oats

- 1 tablespoon cinnamon

- ½ tsp salt

- ½ tsp baking soda

- ½ cup raisins

- ½ cup cranberries

- ¼ chopped walnuts

- ¼ chopped pecans

Here's the step-by-step procedure:

- In a mixing bowl, place room temperature butter brown sugar and granulated sugar. Mix until a smooth consistency form.

- While mixing add the eggs, one at a time, and mix until the eggs are fully incorporated with the butter and sugar then add the vanilla.

- In a separate bowl, place the flour quick cooking oats cinnamon, salt and baking soda.

- Dump the dry ingredients into the butter mixture.

- Mix slowly until the dry ingredients are mix to a smooth consistency. Don't over mix.

- Add raisins and cranberries. Fold them into the mixture.

- I use a scoop to measure out the dough. Press the cookie flat and top with nuts.

- Bake the cookies at 375 degrees for about 6 minutes.

- I take them out of the oven slightly under cooked. This help keep the chewy consistency

Enjoy your delicious homemade oatmeal raisin cookies!

Lemon Zucchini Cookies with a Twist

Note:

These cookies were originally created when I worked at the Columbine Bakery in Avon, Colorado. I have since developed my own unique recipe inspired by the flavors of my Morning Glory muffin. The creaming method is used in this recipe, so make sure all your ingredients are at room temperature.

To make the Lemon Zucchini Cookies, you will need the following:

- 1 cup soft butter
- 1 cup granulated sugar
- 2 tbsp canola or blended oil
- 1 ½ eggs (about 4oz)
- 2 cups all-purpose flour
- ¼ tsp salt
- ½ tsp baking powder
- ½ cup shredded zucchini
- 2 tbsp lemon zest
- ¼ cup shredded carrot

- ¼ cup shredded Granny Smith apple

- ¼ cup unsweetened coconut flakes

- ¼ cup chopped walnuts

Here's the step-by-step procedure:

- In a mixing bowl, cream together the butter, sugar, and oil until smooth and well combined.

- Add the eggs to the mixture and continue to mix until smooth.

- Stir in the lemon zest, shredded zucchini, shredded carrot, shredded apple, coconut flakes, and chopped walnuts.

- In a separate bowl, combine the flour, salt, and baking powder.

- Gradually add the flour mixture to the butter mixture, mixing until just combined.

- Transfer the dough to the refrigerator and chill until it is cool.

- Preheat the oven to 350 degrees.

- Using a cookie scoop or a spoon, drop rounded portions of dough onto a baking sheet. Avoid pressing the dough down.

- Bake the cookies in the preheated oven for about 6 minutes or until lightly golden on the edges.

- Allow the cookies to cool on the baking sheet for a few minutes before transferring them to a wire rack to cool completely.

Enjoy these delicious Lemon Zucchini Cookies with a twist! Perfect for any occasion.

Mouth-watering Brownies

When making brownies from scratch, using top-quality chocolate ingredients is crucial for the best-tasting results. Personally, I prefer using Valrhona brand 66% chocolate and a high-quality Dutch Process Cocoa Powder. There are many other excellent chocolate brands available, so choose one that you trust. Instead of using chocolate chips, I often chop up a bar or coins of chocolate to create a more unique texture. Additionally, lining your pan with parchment paper makes it easier to remove the brownies from the pan.

To make these brownies, you will need:

- 1 cup Dutch Process cocoa powder

- ½ cup melted butter

- 4 eggs

- 2 cups granulated sugar

- ½ cup flour

- ½ cup high-quality chocolate chips

- ½ tsp salt

- ½ tsp vanilla extract

Here's the step-by-step procedure:

- Begin by melting the butter.

- Once the butter is melted, add the salt and vanilla to it.

- Mix the sugar and cocoa powder in a separate bowl.

- Stir the eggs into the melted butter mixture.

- Add the flour to the mixture and mix all the ingredients until you achieve a smooth consistency.

- Fold in high-quality chocolate chips.

- Grease a 9-inch square pan and line it with parchment paper for easy removal.

- Preheat your oven to 350 degrees Fahrenheit.

- Pour the brownie batter into the prepared pan and spread it evenly.

- Bake the brownies in the oven for approximately 20 minutes or until they reach an internal temperature of 180 degrees Fahrenheit.

Following these steps will ensure that you achieve delicious brownies with a rich and indulgent taste. Enjoy!

Muffin Batter Recipe

Note:

Make my favorite Blueberry muffins and other fruit-filled muffins with this batter.

To make the Muffin Batter, you will need:

- 8 oz soft butter

- 12 oz or 1.5 cups granulated sugar

- 3.5 eggs

- 1.5 oz or 3 tbsp honey

- 24 oz or 3 cups all-purpose flour

- 2 tsp salt

- 1.5 tsp baking Soda

- 1.25 cups milk

Here's the step-by-step procedure:

- This is a creaming method. Start with room-temperature butter, sugar, and eggs. Mix the butter and sugar to a smooth consistency.

- Add the eggs and continue mixing until smooth.

- Combine the flour, salt, and baking soda, then gradually add these dry ingredients to the mixture.

- Pour in some milk and mix gently to prevent splashing.

- Gradually add the remainder of the milk while continuing to mix.

- Mix until the batter is smooth, but avoid over-mixing to prevent a dense texture.

- Store the muffin batter in the refrigerator for future use.

Cooking instructions:

- Bake the muffins at 375 degrees for 18-20 minutes.

- Reduce the oven temperature to 300 degrees and bake for an additional 3 minutes.

- Ensure the internal temperature reaches 190-200 degrees.

Instructions for Blueberry Muffins:

- Prepare a muffin tin by lightly spraying it with pan spray.

- Place a muffin cup paper in each cup, spray the paper, and fill the cup halfway with the batter.

- Add five frozen blueberries or your choice of berry/fruit on top of the batter.

- Repeat the filling process for each cup.

- Optionally, top off the muffins with Oatmeal Streusel.

Oatmeal Streusel Recipe

To make these Oatmeal Streusel, you will need:

- 8 oz soft butter

- 4 oz granulated sugar

- 4 oz brown sugar

- 1.5 cups old-fashioned oats

- 1.5 cups all-purpose flour

Here's the step-by-step procedure:

- Mix the butter and sugar until smooth.

- Add the flour and oatmeal, gently mixing until the flour absorbs into the butter.

- If the mixture appears too dry, add a little water.

Chocolate Chip Cookies

Note:

This recipe follows the creaming method. Ensure all ingredients are at room temperature. Adjust baking powder for different elevations.

To make these Chocolate Chip Cookies, you will need:

- 5 oz soft butter
- 5 oz organic palm shortening
- 8 oz brown sugar
- 8 oz granulated sugar
- 3 ½ eggs
- 2 tablespoons agave syrup or honey (optional)
- 1 ½ tablespoons vanilla extract
- 1 tablespoon baking powder (adjust for elevation)
- 20 oz all-purpose flour
- 20 oz chocolate chips

Here's the step-by-step procedure:

- Mix the butter, shortening, sugars, agave syrup (if using), and vanilla until smooth.

- Add the eggs and continue mixing until smooth.

- Gradually incorporate the flour and baking powder, mixing until smooth.

- Refrigerate the dough until cooled.

- Portion the dough evenly and press it down using a scoop.

- Bake at 350 degrees for 6-8 minutes. Adjust baking time for desired texture (slightly undercooked for chewy, longer for crunchy).

Cheesecake

Cheesecake is actually a baked custard that requires careful attention to achieve the desired results. One common technique to ensure a smooth and evenly cooked cheesecake is to cook it in a water bath. However, I have found that adjusting the oven temperature and baking for a longer period of time can achieve similar results. It is important to note that all the ingredients should be at room temperature before starting.

Once the cheesecake is baked, allow it to cool down. For a firmer texture, I personally prefer placing the cake in the freezer. To remove the cake from the pan, gently apply a little heat to the sides, and the cake will easily fall out. At this point, you can choose to decorate the cake or simply cut and serve. Personally, I find that serving it with raspberry sauce adds a delightful touch.

For the cheesecake itself, you will need the following:

- 3 lbs cream cheese

- 1 cup granulated sugar

- ¾ cup sour cream

- 5 whole eggs

- 2 egg yolks

- 3 tablespoons cornstarch
- ¼ cup milk
- 3 tablespoons vanilla extract

Now, let's dive into the procedure:

- Begin by mixing the cream cheese and sugar until you achieve a smooth consistency.
- Then, gradually add the sour cream and ensure it is fully incorporated.
- Continue mixing and add the eggs, one at a time, until all the eggs are well blended.
- Add the vanilla extract to enhance the flavor.
- In a separate bowl, liquify the cornstarch with the milk and carefully add it to the cheesecake mixture.

To bake the cheesecake:

- Use a 10-inch cake pan.
- The cake will soufflé, meaning it will rise during the cooking process. However, as it cools, it will return to its original height in the pan. Fill the pan to about three-quarters height.
- Preheat the oven to 285 degrees and bake the cheesecake for 45-60 minutes.
- To ensure the cheesecake is cooked through, check that the internal temperature reaches at least 150

degrees. Be cautious not to overheat it, as this can curdle the eggs and result in a poor texture.

By following these steps and paying attention to the temperature and cooking time, you can create a delicious and perfectly cooked cheesecake. Enjoy!

Salad Dressing Recipes

Caesar Dressing

Note:

I have two Caesar dressing recipes for you. The first one is eggless or not mayo-based. The second one starts with an egg emulsion that creates a basic mayo base for the dressing. Another way to approach the second dressing is to substitute mayonnaise for the egg yolk, mustard, and oil.

Dressing #1: Eggless Caesar Dressing

This eggless Caesar dressing recipe is perfect for anyone who wants to enjoy the classic flavor of Caesar salad without worrying about the risk of consuming raw eggs. With its tangy and creamy texture, this dressing will satisfy your taste buds and add extra flavor to your salads.

To make the Eggless Caesar Dressing, you will need:

- 4 oz anchovies or anchovy paste
- ½ cup Dijon mustard
- ½ cup lemon juice
- 1 oz Worcestershire sauce
- ½ tablespoon chopped garlic

- 1 ½ cups canola oil

- ½ cup extra virgin olive oil

- Salt and pepper to taste

- 2 oz warm water

Here's the step-by-step procedure:

- To start, prepare all the ingredients. Ensure that the anchovies are cleaned and chopped finely if using fresh ones.

- Combine the anchovies, mustard, lemon juice, Worcestershire sauce, and garlic in a blender. Blend until smooth.

- Gradually add the canola oil and extra virgin olive oil while blending continuously to emulsify the mixture.

- Season with salt and pepper to taste. Add warm water to thin it out if you prefer a lighter dressing.

- Transfer the dressing to a jar or container with a tight-fitting lid. Store in the refrigerator for up to a week.

Enjoy this delicious and savory Anchovy Caesar Dressing on your salads, sandwiches or as a dip for your favorite veggies!

Dressing #2: Classic Caesar Dressing

Caesar dressing is a classic salad dressing that has been people's favorite for decades. It is a creamy, tangy, and flavorful dressing, perfect for any salad.

To make the Classic Caesar Dressing, you will need:

- 1-2 egg yolks
- 1 tablespoon lemon juice
- 1 tablespoon red wine vinegar
- ½ cup olive oil and canola oil blend
- 1-ounce anchovies or anchovy paste
- 1 teaspoon Dijon mustard
- 1 teaspoon Worcestershire sauce
- ¼ cup grated parmesan cheese
- Salt and pepper to taste

Here's the step-by-step procedure:

- In a blender, combine the egg yolks, lemon juice, red wine vinegar, mustard, anchovies, and garlic.
- Slowly add the oil blend while blending the ingredients.
- Fold in the grated parmesan cheese and season with salt and pepper.

- If desired, thin the dressing with water.

Balsamic Dressing

This dressing is the perfect balance of tangy and sweet, and it goes well with just about any salad or dish. Plus, it's effortless to make with just a few simple ingredients.

Note:

Adding fresh herbs to this dressing is optional. I add sugar components because it will brighten up the flavor of the dressing.

To make the Balsamic Dressing, you will need:

- ¼ cup red wine vinegar

- ¼ cup balsamic vinegar

- 1 tablespoon Dijon mustard

- 1 ½ cups blended olive oil and canola oil

- 3 tablespoons fresh herbs (optional: parsley, tarragon, chives)

- ¼ cup sugar

- ¼ cup honey

- Salt and pepper to taste

Here's the step-by-step procedure:

- Place the red wine vinegar, balsamic vinegar, mustard, sugar, honey, and herbs in a blender.

- Gradually add the oil blend while blending the ingredients.

- Season with salt and pepper.

- If needed, thin the dressing with water.

Thousand Island Dressing

A condiment that is widely appreciated and commonly utilized in Rueben sandwiches is the traditional dressing. This dressing has become a popular choice for those seeking to enhance the flavor of their sandwich with a timeless and classic condiment.

To make a delicious sauce, you will need the following ingredients:

- 1 cup of mayonnaise

- 2 oz of prepared chili sauce

- 2 oz of ketchup

- 2 oz of sweet pickle relish

- ¼ cup of finely diced yellow onion

- 1 clove of minced garlic

- 1 tablespoon of Worcestershire sauce

- 1 tablespoon of paprika

- 1 tablespoon of fresh chopped parsley

- Salt and pepper to taste

Here's the step-by-step procedure:

- Finely dice the yellow onion and mince the garlic.

- Chop the fresh parsley.

- In a bowl, combine all the ingredients except for the salt and pepper.

- Season with salt and pepper to taste.

Italian Dressing

For this particular recipe, it is recommended to add a sugar component to the dressing to ensure that all flavors are balanced. Additionally, if the dressing has been refrigerated and appears to have separated, it is important to shake it well before use to ensure it is properly mixed.

Note:

You will see that in this recipe, I use an equal amount of sugar to the acidic components. This is not necessary, but over the years working with this type of dressing, I have found that adding a sugar component creates a much better balance of flavors to the dressing. The dressing will hold in the refrigerator but eventually will separate. If the dressing separates, shake before using.

To make a delicious salad dressing, you will need the following ingredients:

-   ½ small red onion (about 4oz)

-   2 medium garlic cloves (about 1oz)

-   1 oz white wine

-   1 oz red or white wine vinegar

-   1 oz lemon juice

-   1 oz sugar

-   1 oz agave syrup

-   ¾ cup Bloned olive oil

-   1 tablespoon Dijon mustard

-   ½ tablespoon dry thyme

-   ½ tablespoon dry oregano

-   2 tablespoons fresh chopped parsley

-   1 tablespoon fresh chopped basil

-   Salt and pepper to taste

Here's the step-by-step procedure:

-   In a sauté pan, cook the red onion and garlic until slightly golden brown.

-   Add the dry herbs and cook for a minute.

-   Add the white wine and cook until it evaporates.

- Transfer these ingredients to a blender and add the vinegar, lemon juice, sugar, agave syrup, and fresh herbs.

- Blend the ingredients while slowly adding the olive oil.

- Season with salt and pepper.

Blue Cheese Dressing

Blue cheese dressing is a delicious condiment that perfectly pairs perfectly with salads, wings, and many other dishes. Some people prefer their blue cheese dressing to be chunky with larger pieces of cheese, while others prefer a smoother texture. No matter how you like it, blue cheese dressing is a crowd-pleaser that adds flavor to any meal.

To make the Blue Cheese Dressing, you will need:

- 2 cups mayonnaise

- 1 cup sour cream

- ½ cup milk

- ¾-pound blue cheese crumbles

- 2 oz lemon juice

- 2 oz white wine vinegar

- 2 oz granulated sugar

- 1 oz Worcestershire sauce

- 3 tablespoons fresh chopped parsley

- 1 tablespoon Tabasco

- 1 ½ tablespoons kosher salt

- 1 tablespoon freshly ground black pepper

Here's the step-by-step procedure:

- In a large bowl, mix together mayonnaise, sour cream, and milk until well combined.

- Add blue cheese crumbles and stir gently.

- In a separate bowl, whisk together lemon juice, white wine vinegar, sugar, Worcestershire sauce, parsley, Tabasco, kosher salt, and black pepper.

- Pour the whisked mixture into the bowl with the blue cheese and mayo mixture.

- Gently fold all the ingredients together until well combined.

- Cover the bowl with plastic wrap and refrigerate for at least 30 minutes before serving.

This delicious blue cheese dressing is perfect for salads, sandwiches, and as a dip for vegetables or chips. Enjoy!

Ranch Dressing (from scratch)

This homemade ranch dressing has a rich and savory flavor. It is a creamy and flavorful dressing that is perfect for salads, sandwiches, and even as a dip for vegetables. Here's how to make it:

To make the Ranch Dressing, you will need:

- 1 cup mayonnaise
- 1 cup sour cream
- 1 cup buttermilk
- 1 oz lemon juice
- 3 roasted shallots
- 3 roasted garlic cloves
- 1 tablespoon Worcestershire sauce
- ¼ cup chopped parsley
- ¼ cup chopped chives
- 1 tablespoon Dijon mustard
- 1 tablespoon ground celery seed
- 1 tablespoon onion powder
- 1 ½ tablespoons kosher salt
- 1 tablespoon fresh ground black pepper

Here's the step-by-step procedure:

- In a large mixing bowl, combine the mayonnaise, sour cream, and buttermilk. Whisk until smooth.

- Add the lemon juice, Worcestershire sauce, Dijon mustard, ground celery seed, onion powder, kosher salt, and black pepper. Whisk until well combined.

- Finely chop the roasted shallots and roasted garlic cloves and add them to the bowl.

- Add the chopped parsley and chopped chives to the bowl. Stir until all the ingredients are evenly distributed throughout the dressing.

- Cover the bowl with plastic wrap and chill in the refrigerator for at least 30 minutes before serving.

This dressing can be stored in an airtight container in the refrigerator for up to one week. Give it a good stir before serving, as the ingredients may settle over time. Enjoy!

Guacamole

Here's a quick fix for those snack cravings. This recipe comes from a chef I had the pleasure of working with 35 years ago, and he was from Mexico. It's still my go-to recipe for Guac. The key is to use avocados that are at the peak of their ripeness. Overripe or underripe avocados do not make delicious guacamole. The avocados should be firm, but when you press on them, you should feel the flesh will allow a slight impression. This takes a little experience, but you'll learn!

To make the Guac, you will need:

- 3 ripe avocados

- 3 tablespoons finely diced red onion

- 2 tablespoon finely diced tomato

- 1 medium size clove of garlic crushed and minced

- 1 teaspoon finely diced jalapeño

- 1 tablespoon fresh chopped cilantro

- 1 tablespoon fresh lemon juice

- 3 drops of Tabasco

- Salt and pepper to taste

Here's the step-by-step procedure:

- In a bowl, cut open and place avocados.

- Add all your ingredients, leaving the salt and pepper for later.

- Crush with a spoon or whip, but don't over-mix; I like the avocado to be a little chunky.

- Go ahead and add your salt and pepper to taste.

- Refrigerate until needed, and serve.

Waldorf Salad

I was introduced to this salad at my grandmother's house in Staten Island, New York City. My grandparents were members of the New York City Garden Club, and my grandmother would compete in flower arrangements. Back then, the club would meet at the very famous Waldorf Astoria Hotel. There, she had this famous salad, and later on, she'd prepare it for us whenever we would visit. The salad was initially created by Oscar Tschirky, who happened to be the maître d of the hotel.

Fast forward to today in time, so many more varieties of apples are available today as compared to back then. So, I have chosen some non-traditional apples for this recipe.

Here's what you'll need to make the salad:

- 3 peeled honey crisp apples diced ¼ inch

- 3 peeled gala apples diced ¼ inch

- 3 peeled granny smith apples diced ¼ inch

- 1 cup toasted walnuts

- ¾ cup mayonnaise

- ¾ cup sour cream

- 1 teaspoon fresh lemon juice

- 1 teaspoon granulated sugar

- Salt and pepper to taste

Here's the step-by-step procedure:

- Start by toasting your walnuts in an oven at 350 degrees for about 6 minutes.

- Peel and dice your apples and put them in a container with water and a little lemon juice. This will prevent them from turning brown as you go through the peeling process.

- Once all your apples are peeled, place all your ingredients in a bowl and mix. Season with salt and pepper.

- Chill the salad before serving.

- Serve on a bed of iceberg lettuce, just like Grandmother would!

Country Style Potato Salad

Here's what you'll need to make the salad:

- 2 ½ lbs. cooked russet potato

- ¼ cup apple cider vinegar

- ¼ cup granulated sugar

- ¼ cup Dijon mustard

- ½ cup mayonnaise

- ½ cup yellow onion

- ½ cup finely diced celery

- ¼ cup sweet pickle relish

- 3 hard-boiled eggs

- 2 tablespoons of fresh parsley, chopped

- 2 garlic cloves

- Salt and pepper to taste

Note:

A very important part of making this salad. I cook the potatoes peeled and whole or cut in half. Once the potato is tender and removed from the hot water, you will cut the potato into approximately one-inch cubes while the potato is still warm. You mix the warm potato with the vinegar solution, some salt and pepper, mustard, and mayonnaise.

Due to the fact the potato is warm, the pores in the potato are open and will absorb the flavors from the dressing. This really helps create an amazing flavor profile with your salad.

Here's the step-by-step procedure:

- Cook your potato in boiling water; you can put the potato in the water before it starts to boil.

- Bring your water to a boil before you put the eggs in it. Use a pair of tongs to place the eggs in the boiling water. Cook for 18 minutes. Cool eggs right away and peel.

- While the potato cooks, dice your onion and garlic. Sauté for a minute in olive oil.

- Dice your celery ¼ inch.

- Chop your parsley.

- Slice your eggs.

- Once the potato is cooked, cut them up while they are still warm and add your vinegar, sugar, mustard, mayonnaise, salt and pepper. Fold together gently.

- Add the remaining ingredients and fold again.

- Spread the salad out on a pan about 2 inches high and refrigerate immediately to cool it down.

- Once the salad is cold, you can put it in a storage container and serve it!

Brenner's Family Tomato-based Restaurant Salsa

This recipe was awarded a blue ribbon at the Eagle County Colorado Fair and Rodeo in the professional category. Salsa can be very simple; it's crushed and made into a puree of tomato with a little seasoning. Or it can be a little bit more complex with multiple ingredients. My recipe is more on the complex side. I use a combination of red bell pepper, Anaheim green pepper, and jalapeño pepper.

Here's what you'll need:

- 28 ounces of high-quality crushed tomatoes

- 1 red bell pepper

- 1 Anaheim green pepper

- 1 medium-sized jalapeño

- 1 cup finely diced yellow onion

- 2 medium-sized fresh garlic cloves, crushed and chopped finely

- 2 tablespoons of fresh cilantro, chopped

- 1 tablespoon ground cumin

- 1 teaspoon ground coriander

- Salt and pepper to taste

Here's the step-by-step procedure:

- Sear the skin at a very high temperature so you can peel the skin off the pepper, and the pepper ends up in a cooked state. To sear the skin, you can char the skin on or under a broiler or charbroiler. Another method is cooking the peppers in very hot oil in a pot on the stove. With either method, once your peppers are seared, store them in a container and seal the top for a few minutes. This will steam the skin so it peels off easily.

- Chop the peppers or puree in a food processor.

- Make a puree of about ⅓ of the crushed tomatoes.

- Mix all the ingredients and season with salt and pepper.

- Serve and enjoy!

Chicken Avocado Salad

This is a very simple salad. I had it on my menu at Brenner's for the entire eight years. I credit the success to always making it with very fresh ingredients. The chicken is grilled to order, then sliced and served warm on top of the salad.

Here's what you'll need:

- 1 6 ounces of marinated and grilled chicken breast

- 1 cup chopped Romaine lettuce

- 1 cup chopped iceberg lettuce

- ½ of an avocado sliced

- 1 tablespoon diced red onion

- 3 tomato wedges

- Your choice of dressing or a simple combination of extra virgin olive oil, fresh squeezed lemon juice, salt, and pepper.

Here's the step-by-step procedure:

- Marinate chicken in white wine, fresh chopped garlic, thyme, rosemary, salt and pepper for two hours.

- Cut the lettuce into one-inch size pieces and put on a chilled plate.

- Cut slices in the halved avocado and scoop them out of its skin.

- Sprinkle red onion onto lettuce.

- Place your avocado on top of the lettuce.

- Grill the chicken slice and place it on top of the avocado.

- Place tomato around the plate.

- Add dressing and serve.

Caesar Salad

Over the past three decades, Caesar Salad has been a staple on every lunch and dinner menu I've worked with. It's also one of my personal favorites. During the eight years I ran Brenner's, it remained a constant on my menu. Although there are several Caesar dressing recipes available, I often prefer the one emulsified with egg yolks. Most Caesar salads are quite similar, so to make mine unique, I use homemade croutons and garnish with fresh tomato wedges.

Caesar Salad Recipe:

- 20 oz of fresh chopped Romaine lettuce (preferably organic)

- ¾ cup freshly grated Parmesan cheese

- 2-3 oz Caesar dressing

- 1 ½ cups freshly prepared croutons

- Freshly ground pepper and kosher salt to taste

Instructions:

- Wash (if necessary) and dry the chopped romaine lettuce.

- In a bowl, combine romaine lettuce with dressing.

- Season with freshly ground pepper and a pinch of salt.

- Garnish the salad with croutons and tomato wedges.

Pete's Garlic and Parmesan Croutons Recipe:

- 1 six-inch French baguette, cut into 1 1/2-inch cubes

- 2 tbsp melted butter

- 2 tbsp blended olive oil

- 2 cloves fresh garlic, crushed and chopped

- ¼ cup grated Parmesan cheese

- 1 tsp paprika

- Salt and pepper to taste

Instructions:

- Dice the bread into cubes.

- In a mixing bowl, combine bread cubes with all other ingredients.

- Bake at 350°F for 6-8 minutes.

- Wait until the croutons turn golden brown.

Special Occasion Fruit Salad

I created this salad during the years I had my restaurant, and it has been a staple at holiday events and special occasions. The transformative ingredient is Grand Marnier, which, combined with freshly whipped cream, elevates this dish. I recommend cutting fruits into one-inch cubes; however, melon and pineapple shapes don't have to be perfect.

Fruit Salad Recipe:

- 1 cup cantaloupe melon

- 1 cup honeydew melon

- 1 cup pineapple

- ½ cup fresh blueberries

- ½ cup sliced strawberries

- ½ cup raspberries

- 2 tbsp. Grand Marnier

- 1 tbsp. granulated sugar

- 1 ½ cups fresh whipped cream

Procedure:

- Dice cantaloupe, honeydew, and pineapple into one-inch cubes.

- Slice strawberries.

- In a large bowl, mix diced melon, pineapple, and strawberries.

- Add sugar and Grand Marnier to the fruit mixture; marinate for 30 minutes.

- Gently fold in whipped cream.

- Garnish with blueberries and raspberries before serving.

Spinach Salad

This salad was created for the Chaparral Club House menu in Cordillera, Edwards, Colorado, during the summer of 2002. What I love about this salad is the combination of cold and warm ingredients. It features a spinach base topped with warm, herb-crusted, fried goat cheese and is served with balsamic dressing. This is a plated salad, and I will demonstrate how to create one plate.

Spinach Salad Ingredients:

- 2 oz fresh baby spinach

- A few thinly sliced red onion pieces

- Oven-roasted tomato wedges

- Roasted garlic

- 1 warm slice of herb-crusted goat cheese

- 1-2 tsp balsamic dressing

Herb-Crusted Goat Cheese Preparation:

- Begin with a cylinder-shaped piece of goat cheese. Slice it into ¼- ½ inch slices using butcher string or fishing line.

- Lay the slices on a tray lined with parchment paper and freeze them.

- Use bread crumbs and some dry Italian mix for coating.

- Prepare seasoned all-purpose flour with salt and pepper, and create an egg wash by mixing an egg with a pinch of salt.

- Dredge each frozen goat cheese slice in flour, then the egg wash, then coat with bread crumbs. Freeze dressed slices. Fry them in a pan with canola oil just before serving the salad.

Procedure:

- Cut a roma tomato into quarters and toss in olive oil, salt, and pepper. Roast in the oven at 300°F for 20 minutes until slightly dried out. Cool before use.

- Cook a garlic clove in a pot with a little blended oil until it reaches a light golden brown color; remove from pan.

- Thinly slice red onion.

- Toss spinach with dressing.

- Garnish the salad with roasted tomato, garlic, and red onion.

- Fry the goat cheese and place it on top of the salad.

Appetizers

Throughout my career in the food service industry, I have encountered an enormous variety of appetizer options. These range from simple cheese plates to charcuterie, including cured meats and sausages. Seafood appetizers, such as crab cakes, shrimp cocktails, oysters, and a variety of hot and cold meats, poultry, and vegetables are also popular choices. Typically, the items consist of one or two bites, with several displayed on a plate. In a buffet-style setting, the appetizers are served on platters with a wide array of options. A grand buffet often incorporates all of these elements, along with canapés and Japanese sushi rolls. In this article, I will share several items I have worked with over the years.

There is an incredible variety of methods used to create cheese. As someone who is a fan of all types of cheese, I highly recommend diving deep into the subject by reading *Cheese Primer* by Steven Jenkins. This book offers detailed descriptions of cheeses from around the world.

Here are some of my favorites: Italian Cheeses – Domestic Cheese, Fontina, Havarti, Taleggio, Dill Havarti, Gorgonzola, Blue Cheese Crumbles, Burrata – Tillamook Cheddar, Grana Padano Gouda, Provolone Maytag, Asiago, Mozzarella Di Bufala Spanish Cheese, Pecorino Romano, Parmigiano Reggiano Manchego, Mozzarella Mahon, and Cabrales

Amongst the French variants, I'll recommend Roquefort, Munster, Emmenthal, Camembert, Brie de Meaux, Saint-Andre, Boursin, Comte, Goat Cheese, Raclette, Reblochon, Port Salut

Here is a list of Charcuterie Meats:

- Prosciutto

- Mortadella

- Genoa salami

- Sopressata

- Ham Varieties

- Sausage Varieties

To create an appetizer Charcuterie platter, use the 3 3 3 3 rule: 3 meats, 3 cheeses, 3 starches, and 3 accompaniments.

Some starch ideas include cracker varieties, breadsticks, crostinis, and some bread varieties.

For accompaniments, consider olives varieties, nut varieties, fresh fruit, pickles, spreads, honey varieties, jams and spreads.

More About Appetizers

When planning menus for parties, it's essential to consider popular first-course options. Here are some common selections:

Fruit Platters:

Typically, you'll remove the skin and seeds from the fruits before cutting them into slices or cubes. Arrange the fruits attractively and garnish with berries. Remember to wash whole fruits before peeling. Common fruits include cantaloupe, honeydew melon, casaba melon, watermelon, pineapple, papaya, mango, oranges, grapefruit, kiwi, star fruit, strawberries, blueberries, raspberries, and blackberries.

Crudités Vegetable Plates and Platters:

These consist of raw vegetables served with various dips like ranch dressing, hummus, cheese dip, or sour cream-based dips. Wash produce before preparation and cut into bite-sized pieces or stick shapes. Common vegetables include cherry tomatoes, carrots, mushrooms, yellow squash, broccoli, celery, jicama, blanched asparagus, cauliflower, radish green onions, cucumbers, bell peppers, and zucchini.

Seafood and Smoked/Cured Fish and Seafood:

Serve these items on ice or chilled plates/platters with accompanying sauces like cocktail sauce, tartar sauce, remoulade sauce, mignonette sauce, and fresh lemons.

Options include:

- Cooked shrimp

- Crab claws

- Mussels

- Clams

- Oysters

- Lobster

- Octopus

- Poached salmon

- Squid calamari

- Smoked salmon

- Smoked oysters

- Cooked smoked herring

- Fish eggs

- Caviar

Throughout my career working as a Garde Manger specializing in cold cuisine, I've been inspired by books such as *Garde Manger: The Art and Craft of the Cold*

Kitchen published by John Wiley and Sons Inc., which have been invaluable in shaping my culinary journey.

As we move forward in our exploration of appetizers, I'd like to share some of my favorite menu items, including hot and cold dishes made from meat, seafood, and vegetables crafted into one- or two-bite servings to tantalize your taste buds. These appetizers can be passed or plated and include tomato bruschetta, salmon pinwheels, beef tenderloin, Ahi tuna, shrimp cocktail, crab cakes, oyster, Rockefeller and chicken, and spinach in filo dough.

Appetizers are often served as hors d'oeuvres, typically presented as one-bite items. Some dishes are presented in this style, while others are plated for à la carte dining. To create appealing bite-sized appetizers, think of a base, body, and garnish. The base could be a crostini, cracker, or sliced vegetable like cucumber. Consider a deviled egg as an example: the cooked egg is the base, and it's topped with a flavored filling and garnished with fresh herbs, fish eggs, chopped bacon, etc. The goal is to create a flavor profile that pleases the palate and stimulates cravings for the next course of the meal.

Hors d'oeuvres Recipes:

Deviled Eggs

Ingredients:

- 4 hard-boiled egg yolks
- 4 egg whites
- 2 tbsp mayonnaise
- 1 tsp soft butter
- ½ tsp Dijon mustard
- 2 drops Tabasco sauce
- Salt and pepper to taste
- **Garnish options:** fresh herbs, bacon pieces, lobster chunks

Procedure:

- In a bowl, mix all ingredients until smooth.
- Spoon the yolk mixture back into the egg whites.
- Garnish and serve.

Many hors d'oeuvres use bases like crostini, crackers, or fried wonton wrappers. To make crostinis from baguettes or pre-sliced bread, cut bread into small one- or two-bite pieces for serving. Crackers can be store-bought or homemade using flour, oil, and salt; try searching online for additional ideas like Lavash.

Other base options include sliced vegetables such as cucumbers, celery, mushroom caps, and Belgian endive. Use your imagination and have fun creating different appetizer bases!

Salmon Pinwheels, Beef tenderloin Canapé, Ahi Tuna on a Wonton Crisp

During my time at the Cascade Hotel in Vail, I frequently made these dishes while working in the banquet department, which contributed to the hotel's annual eight million dollars in food revenue. As the head of the cold food section, I helped create tens of thousands of Hors d'oeuvres.

Salmon Pinwheel:

4 oz Scottish smoked salmon, thinly sliced

4 oz cream cheese

1 tsp. fresh chopped dill weed

-   1 tbsp. chopped capers

-   Whole grain crackers

Procedure:

Soften the cream cheese.

Chop the dill weed and capers.

Lay out two sheets of plastic wrap.

Arrange the salmon on one sheet, creating a flat 4x6-inch rectangle.

Spread softened cream cheese over the salmon.

Sprinkle dill and capers onto the cream cheese layer.

Roll salmon into a cylinder using plastic wrap as a
   guide.

Freeze the roll until firm.

Slice the roll into ¼-inch slices.

Place slices on whole-grain crackers.

-    Once softened, garnish with fresh dill.

Beef Tenderloin Canapé:

Note:

You will need a 1½ - 2-inch diameter cylindrical piece
of tenderloin and pre-prepared crostini.

Ingredients:

Beef tenderloin, salted and peppered

A little oil for searing

Prepared horseradish sauce (drain excess water and
   mix with sour cream)

Sprigs of parsley for garnishing

Procedure:

Sear beef in a pan with a little oil until it reaches an internal temperature of 125°F.

Let the beef rest for ten minutes.

Slice beef into ¼-inch thick slices.

Place beef slices on crostini.

Spoon a small amount of horseradish cream on top.

- Garnish with a sprig of parsley.

Ahi Tuna on Wonton Crisps:

To make wonton crisps, cut wonton wrappers into 1.5-inch circles or squares. Fry them in oil heated to 300-350 degrees until golden brown. For the Ahi tuna, cut 4-6oz of tuna into 4-5-inch long and 1.5-inch square pieces. Coat the tuna in Japanese seven-spice Togarashi, with extra sesame seeds added. Sear the tuna in sesame oil with a touch of sugar, ensuring the center remains raw. Create a sauce using sweet Thai chili sauce, soy sauce, mirin wine, rice wine, and sugar, thickened with cornstarch.

To assemble, slice the cooked tuna using a sharp knife and place on the wonton crisps. Add sauce on top and garnish with fresh cilantro.

Shrimp Cocktail:

During my years working in the Garde Manger kitchen, shrimp cocktails frequently showed up on the menu. To cook shrimp, I use a court-bouillon, a French term for seasoned cooking broth.

Ingredients:

1 pound of raw 21-25 count shrimp

2 quarts of water

1 cup roughly chopped yellow onion

½ cup roughly chopped celery

½ cup roughly chopped carrot

½ bunch of parsley

2 bay leaves

6 black peppercorns

- 1 tbsp Kosher salt

Procedure:

Bring water to a boil and add all ingredients except for shrimp. Bring to a boil again before adding the shrimp. Cook shrimp for 2-3 minutes and immediately cool in ice water. Serve with cocktail sauce.

Tomato Bruschetta

Tomato Bruschetta was another hors d' oeuvres I would prepare often while working at the Cascade Village. Mostly, it's grilled bread with garlic oil but you can use some variations. I used focaccia bread slices that were three inches long and ¼ inches wide. Next I would brush it with garlic-flavored oil and bake the sliced bread in the oven until the edges would just start to turn brown. If you see the garlic turning brown, don't flame it further. Allow the garlic to cool down. Furthermore, place the tomato in boiling water until you see the skin leave the flesh. Remove the skin and cut the tomato in half. Squeeze the seeds and water out for the tomato. Don't apply too much force when doing this because you will end up dicing the tomato. A fun way to serve this at home is to put the tomato mixture in a bowl with the crostini on the side.

Tomato Bruschetta

2 slices of grilled or baked focaccia bread

2 - 3 medium size ripe tomatoes

2 medium size cloves of garlic

3 tbsp olive oil

3 large basil leaves

Salt and pepper to taste

Procedure:

Prepare the garlic oil.

Brush your bread with the oil.

Bake or grill.

Concassé and dice your tomato.

Chop your garlic.

Chop your basil.

- Mix all ingredients and season with salt and pepper.

Crab Cakes

There are many variations on Crab Cakes but I prefer it simple. Most supermarkets have lump crab meat, backfire, or claw meat. I prefer Jumbo Lump crab meat for crab cakes, but it is expensive. However, you can use any crab meat. Crab cakes are usually served with sauces. I prefer the Remoulade Sauce.

Maryland Style Crab Cakes with Remoulade Sauce

1 pound well-drained Jumbo Lump crab meat

¼ cup mayonnaise

1-2 eggs

½ cup Ritz Cracker crumbs

1 tbsp Dijon mustard

1 tbsp Fresh chopped parsley

1 tsp. Worcestershire sauce

1 tsp. lemon juice

- Salt and pepper to taste

Procedure

Drain the crab meat.

If needed, crush up the crackers.

Whip your egg, mustard, Worcestershire sauce, and chopped parsley together.

Mix the crab meat with mayonnaise and cracker crumbs. Add egg mixture.

Add the lemon juice and season with salt and pepper.

Form your cakes. I use a 2oz scoop, then press the cakes.

- Fry your cakes to 165 degrees internal temperature.

Remoulade Sauce

1 cup mayonnaise

1 tbsp Dijon mustard

1 tbsp Hungarian Paprika

1 tbsp fresh chopped parsley

2 tsp. lemon juice

2 tsp. sweet pickle relish

½ tsp. fresh chopped garlic

3 drops Tabasco sauce

Portobello Fries

For me, these fries are very reminiscent of the Four Star Chop House at the Cascade Village in Vail, Colorado. I have always been a mushroom lover. If you are familiar with the old-school fried domestic mushrooms at TGI Fridays, this delicacy is for you.

Portobello Fries

2-3 cleaned Portobello mushrooms sliced ½ inch thick

1 cup seasoned flour

Salt and pepper to taste

2 cups tempura batter

- 2 cups canola oil 350 degree

Tempura Batter:

1 cup all-purpose flour

1 tbsp cornstarch

1 large egg

- 1 cup ice-cold water

Heat a pot of canola oil. Make sure you have a specialized thermometer for frying pans. Also, don't heat the oil too much. Furthermore, don't put too many fries in the oil, as it will overcrowd the pan. You can use tweezers to lift the fries.

Procedure

Coat your sliced mushroom in seasoned flour.

Place the strip into the tempura batter and then into the hot oil.

Cook until the fries are golden brown.

Place cooked strips on a paper towel and allow excess oil to drain off.

- Serve with tempura sauce.

Spinach Artichoke Dip

This recipe reminds me of the time I spent working at Gore Range Brewery in Edwards, Colorado. It was served with baked flour and tortilla chips. I prefer it with sliced baguette bread. The base for this dip ia a béchamel sauce, which is basically thickened milk with a roux.

Spinach Artichoke Dip

2 tbsp olive oil

1 large clove chopped

1 36oz package fresh spinach chopped

1 14oz can quartered artichokes

8 oz cream cheese

8 oz shredded mozzarella cheese

4 oz parmesan reggiano shaved

1 qt béchamel sauce

-   Salt and pepper to taste

Béchamel Sauce

5 tbsp butter

1/4 cup all-purpose flour

1 quart milk

- ¼ tsp. nutmeg

Procedure

Add nutmeg and flour to melted butter.

Stir and cook until it is golden brown.

- Heat your milk on a low flame and whisk while it cooks.

Spinach Artichoke Dip

Add your cheese to the béchamel and cook on low flame.

If you have an emersion blender, use it to blend the mixture. Otherwise, cook on low heat until the cheese has melted and is fairly smooth.

Add chopped spinach and cook for a few minutes.

Add artichokes and cook for two more minutes.

Season the concoction with salt and pepper.

Serve with bread or tortillas on the side.

Oyster Bienville/Rockefeller

I was introduced to these two appetizers in 1983 while I was working as a chef at the Riverton Country Club. Our director for food and beverages was a renowned Chef in South Jersey and the Philadephia area. I had the unique privilege of working with him for seven months. There were some amazing items on the menu, but these two got me hooked. My family has always had a thing for eating seafood. As luck would have it, throughout my career, I got to work a lot with seafood. These oyster items are best prepared with fresh oysters, but you can use frozen ones as well.

Oysters Rockefeller

One dozen oysters on the half-shell

12 tsp. olive oil

¼ cup yellow onion finely diced

1 clove of fresh garlic

6 oz fresh spinach chopped

2 oz cream cheese

3 tbsp heavy cream

1 tbsp Pernod anise liquor

3 tbsp Parmesan reggiano

2 tbsp melted butter

¼ cup bread crumbs

- Salt and pepper to taste

Procedure

Detach and rinse the oyster, and return it to the shell.

Saute onions and garlic in the olive oil.

Add your fresh chopped spinach.

Add the heavy cream, cream cheese, and Pernod. Cook to a smooth consistency.

Put a tablespoon of the spinach mixture on each ouster.

Mix your bread crumbs and parmesan cheese with the melted butter.

Sprinkle the oysters with the breadcrumb mixture, salt, and pepper.

- Cook oysters until they are golden brown.

Oyster Bienville

1 dozen oysters

1 tbsp olive oil

¼ cup chopped mushrooms

¼ cup chopped fresh shrimp

¼ cup Finley diced yellow onion

1 clove finely chopped garlic

3 tbsp heavy cream

2oz cream cheese

1 tbsp Sherry wine

1 tsp. lemon juice

2 tbsp melted butter

¼ cup bread crumbs

3 tbsp grated parmesan cheese

Salt and pepper

Coconut Shrimp

This is a great shrimp item, and I got to work on it a lot between the years 2000 and 2010. However, it has somewhat disappeared. Basically, it is a combination of deep-fried shrimp, bread crumbs, and coconut flakes. I would usually serve it with sweet Thai chili sauce.

Coconut Shrimp

1 dozen shrimp

1 cup seasoned flour

Egg wash, 2 eggs, and a sprinkle of salt

1 cup panko bread crumbs

1 cup shredded sweet coconut

Salt and pepper to taste

- 2 cups canola oil for frying

Procedure

Peel and cut the shrimps in a way that they lay out flat.

Dip the shrimp into the egg wash, followed by seasoned flour.

Dip the shrimps into the egg again, followed by breadcrumbs.

Carefully fry the shrimps at 350 degrees.

Don't overcrowd the oil with too many shrimps.

Serve with sweet Thai chili sauce.

Soups

When I was a child, I would often see my mother and my grandmother preparing different kinds of soups. Therefore, soups were a staple component of our lunch and breakfast menus. Working as a saucier, I got the chance to prepare various soups, broths, and stocks. To prepare the stocks, I would often butcher different types of meats. It was around this point that I fully discovered French cuisine, and completely fell in love with it.

Clam Chowder

2 10oz cans of chopped clams

2 10oz cans of clam juice

2 cups heavy cream

2 cups ¼ inch diced russet potatoes

1 cup ¼ inch diced yellow onion

1 cup ¼ inch diced celery

½ cup whole butter

3 tbsp blended oil

½ cup all-purpose flour

1 tbsp chopped fresh garlic

2 tbsp fresh chopped parsley

1 tsp. dry thyme

3 bay leaves

- Salt and pepper to taste

Procedure

Dice the russet potato.

Dice your onion and celery, and chop your garlic and parsley.

Use a heavy bottom 1-gallon pot, melt the butter, and add oil.

Add the potatoes, celery, onions and garlic, thyme, and bay leaves. Cook for a few minutes.

Add flour and cook for a couple more minutes.

Add the clam juice and heavy cream.

Bring to a simmer and cook until the potatoes are soft.

Add the chopped clams and chopped parsley.

Season with salt and pepper.

If you think the chowder needs to be a little thicker, use cornstarch to thicken the soup.

- Liquify a couple of tablespoons of cornstarch with water and add to the simmering soup.

French Onion

French onion soup is my favorite. Caramelized onion is the secret to the robust flavor of this soup. The combination of butter and salt aid the caramelization process. Milk fats also aid the process. You can use any type of onion, depending on their availability. Personally, I prefer the yellow onions. While working at the Bennigan's Tavern, I would use a recipe that starts with slicing the onions. To get the right consistency, I like using a combination of chicken and beef broth.

French Onion Soup

3 pounds of yellow onions sliced half-inch

1/4 cup olive oil blend

1/4 cup whole butter

1 tbsp Kosher salt

1 tsp. dry thyme

1 tsp fresh ground black pepper

3 bay leaves

1 cup good red wine

1 tbsp Dry sherry

1 quart beef stock/broth

1 quart chicken stock/broth

Sliced French bread toasted

Shredded Gruyere cheese

- Shredded mozzarella cheese

Procedure

Slice your onion ½ inch slices.

Put the oil, butter, thyme, salt, and black pepper in a 1-gallon pot.

Start on high heat.

Once the butter has melted, add the onions.

Cook the onions on high to medium heat, stirring regularly for about 45 minutes until the onions get a nice golden brown color to them.

Deglaze the onions with the red wine and sherry.

Add the stock/broth.

Simmer for thirty minutes.

Soup is ready. Put the soup in a bowl and topped with toasted bread and shredded cheese.

Melt the cheese until it starts to brown.

- Serve soup on an underliner plate.

Cream of Mushroom Soup

I have been making cream of mushroom soup throughout my career. Some of the other soups I have prepared are creamed carrot ginger, creamed spinach, creamed potato, and creamed cauliflower. To make sure a soup, you need an emersion blender. While most people use the domestic button mushroom, feel free to use any type of mushroom.

Ingredients

3 20z domestic button mushrooms sliced

1 large yellow onion ¼ inch diced

1-2 tbsp Fresh chopped garlic

1 tsp. dry thyme

3 bay leaves

1/2 cup whole butter

1/4 cup blended olive oil

3/4 cup all-purpose flour

5 cups good chicken stock/broth

2 cups heavy cream

1 good white wine

-    Salt and pepper to taste

Procedure

Place your butter and oil in a 1-gallon heavy bottom pot.

Add your mushrooms, onion, thyme, bay leaf, and a little salt and pepper.

Cook the mixture for about five minutes, caramelizing the onion and mushrooms.

Add the garlic and continue cooking for about two minutes so the garlic blossoms.

Add your flour and continue cooking for a couple more minutes.

Add your white wine first, then your stock and heavy cream.

Simmer for twenty minutes.

Blend your soup.

Chicken Tortilla Soup

I discovered this after I moved to Colorado Vail, then Eagle, and present in Edwards, Colorado. Before Colorado became a state, it was a territory of Mexico. Due to that fact, Colorado has always had a strong Mexican food culture. I feel very fortunate to start working with so many amazing ingredients earlier on in my career. One of the items I learned to prepare is the chicken tortilla soup. The primary ingredient you will need prior to making the soup is tortilla chips. In a professional kitchen, we have a large fryer that makes it easy to make these chips. If you're buying tortilla chips at a supermarket, get the ones with little or no salt. Usually, the chicken meat is in a precooked form, but you can do it with raw chicken. However, the latter takes longer. With this recipe, the chicken comes from a pre-roasted chicken available at your supermarket.

Ingredients

Chicken meat from one roast chicken, white and dark meat chopped

1 medium size yellow onion ¼ inch dice

1 small green bell pepper ¼ inch dice

1 small red bell pepper ¼ inch dice

1 cup diced Anaheim green chilis

1 tbsp fresh chopped garlic

1 tbsp Ground cumin

1 tbsp smoked paprika

1 tsp. Light chili powder

1 tsp. ground coriander

2 quarts good chicken stock/broth

1/4 cup blended olive oil

Salt and pepper to taste

- 2 hands full of tortilla chips slightly crushed

Procedure

Use a one-gallon heavy bottom pot and add your oil.

Place your onions and pepper in the pot and cook until they are soft

Add your garlic and seasoning and cook for two minutes.

Add the chicken meat and continue cooking for a minute.

Add the chicken stock and simmer for ten minutes.

- Add your crushed tortillas and season with salt and pepper.

Smoked Pheasant Soup with Wild Rice and Roasted Corn

This soup was introduced to me when I was training in the saucier area at Westin Hotel in the Cascade Village in Vail Colorado. During those five years, I made the rounds through the brigade system. You might have a hard time finding smoked pheasant. I would suggest looking at a high-end butcher shop or specialty market. Another approach is to use smoked chicken. You need to have precooked wild rice due to the fact that wild rice takes a long time to cook. If you have a smoker grill such as a Trager, you can cook the pheasant in your backyard. This soup requires smoked pheasant stock. In our hotel, we bought pre-cooked smoked pheasant breast. We would remove the meat and used bones to create the stock. Another pre-cooked item in the soup is roasted corn.

Ingredients

2 pounds smoked pheasant meat ¼ inch diced

2 quarts smoked pheasant stock

1 quart heavy cream

1 cup yellow onion ¼ inch dice

1 cup celery ¼ inch dice

2 cups roasted corn kernels

2 cup cooked wild rice

1 cup apple juice

1/4 cup cider vinegar

1/4 cup brown sugar

1/4 cup sesame oil

1 tbsp liquid smoke

1 tbsp Tabasco

-   Salt and pepper to taste

Procedure

Use a one-gallon heavy bottom pot and add sesame oil.

Cook onions and celery until they are soft.

Add pheasant meat and corn. Cook for five minutes.

Add remaining ingredients and season with salt and
pepper.

Cook soup at a low temperature for 20 minutes.

Grains and Rice

There are several similarities between cooking rice and grains. In both cases, you will combine the grain or rice with water. Bring it to a boil until the water is absorbed. You can add a small amount of salt to cooking grains and rice, but make sure not to add too much salt. Usually, what I do to cook grains or rice is to put the rice or grain in a shallow but deep pan. Then I cover the pan with oven-safe plastic wrap followed by an aluminum foil. I poke a few holes through the aluminum foil because I cook with convection heat, and the holes help prevent the air circulation from blowing off the foil. Cooking your rice and grains for 30-40 minutes at 350 degrees heat is ideal. Most people prefer doing it on a stove, but I prefer using an oven.

Vegetables and Root Vegetables

Fresh vegetables add to the glory of your meal. When cooked properly, they add color, texture, and nutrition to your plate. To make the most of your vegetables, make sure not to overcook them. Their nutritional value is actually best in the raw state, but most of us are more accustomed to the cooked texture. If you ask me, I usually prepare the veggies before plating the meal. I reheat them before serving.

Center of the Plate Proteins, Meats, Fish and Seafood, Vegetables

So, over the years cooking professionally, I have had the pleasure of preparing a very wide variety of these items. These proteins belong in the center of our plate. So, how do we cook these items? The answer depends on what you're trying to cook. Some of the best ways to prepare these proteins are poaching, deep frying, stewing, steaming, moist heat cooking, roasting, boiling, and pan frying.

Sauces

In my opinion, most main dish courses are better complimented by a sauce. A sauce enhances and accents the flavor of the food. It is a great way to introduce another level of flavor profile to a dish. Here are some sauces you should be familiar with. Some common types of sauces are as follows

Béchamel

Hollandaise

Tomato Sauce

Hot Sauce

Pesto

Mayonnaise

Barbecue

Soy

Teriyaki

Tartar

Aioli

Romesco

Bolognese

Alfredo

Piccata

Veloute

Demi Glaze/ Brown Sauce

Entrées

Here is a list of entrées and cultural styles of cuisine I have worked with over the past decades. My book is not a full-blown cookbook. My intention with this list is to provide you with ideas that you might consider making in your kitchen. I will create a few recipes to demonstrate my approach to preparing an entrée menu item. Recipes most, if not all, of these items can be found on the internet. I'm in the process of creating my own cooking channel where I will be doing cooking demonstrations with many of these items. For now, I leave you with a couple of recipes.

Poached Lobster New England Clam Bake

Herb Crusted Lamb Chops

Prime Rib standing Rib Roast Peanut Crusted Lamb Chops

New York Strip Steak Curried Lamb Stew

Beef Tenderloin with Peppercorn sauce Enchilada Casseroles

Beef Stroganoff Braised Flat Iron Steak

Philly Cheese Steak, Chicken Fried Steak

Ruben Sandwich Halibut with Lemon Butter

Monte Cristo Roast Pork Tenderloin

Chicken Alfredo Braised Flank Steak

Chicken Piccata Chicken Cordon Blue

Chicken Marsala Linguine with Clam sauce

Blackened Salmon Herb and Peppercorn Crusted Sword
  Fish

Shrimp Scampi Grilled Veal Chop

Baked Cod Fish Pan Seared Duck Breast

Seafood in Wine and Lemon Butter Crispy Duck

Shepherd's Pie Chicken Parmesan

Chicken Pot Pie Asian Style, Chinese

Salmon Wrapped in Puff Pastry Asian Style Japanese

Seared Diver Scallops Asian Style Vietnamese

Spaghetti Bolognese Middle Eastern Cusine

Hamburger Variations Chicken Cacciatore

Fried Chicken Short Ribs

Marinated Grilled Chicken Breast

Oven Roasted Chicken

Baby Back Ribs

Oven Roasted Turkey

Wild Game Venison

-Wild Game Elk

-Wild Game Rabbit

Wild Game Boar

PETER C BRENNER

French and Italian Pastas, German Austrian Style
Cuisine

240

Chicken Marsala

I first experienced Chicken Marsala when my mother would make it for us while we were growing up. It is a classic Italian-American delicacy, slightly sweet and savory. You can sauté a whole chicken breast as a shortcut. I like its scallopine style. You slice the chicken breast into three equal parts. Then, place the pieces between plastic wraps and pound them with a kitchen mallet about a ¼ inch of thickness.

Ingredients

2-3 boneless chicken breast

1/4 cup finely diced onion

3 cloves of fresh chopped garlic

8oz sliced mushrooms

4 tbsp Blended olive oil

3 tbsp unsalted butter

1 cup chicken stock/broth

3/4 cup good marsala wine

3/4 cup heavy cream

1/2 tsp dry thyme

1 tbsp fresh chopped Parsley

1/2 cup flour

Salt and pepper to taste

Procedure

Slice and pound your chicken breast.

Season your flour with some salt and pepper.

Have a pan ready with the oil and butter hot.

You want your pan temperature to be toward the very hot 375 degrees.

Dip your chicken scallops in the flour and then put them into the hot pan.

Don't overcrowd the pan. The chicken will cook quickly, and then you will remove the Chicken from the pan.

Add your onions, mushrooms, thyme, and parsley to the pan and cook them for about two minutes.

Continually stir the ingredients while they cook. Then add the garlic and cook for 1 minute.

Add your marsala wine and let it reduce for two minutes, then add your heavy cream.

Return the chicken to the pan. Once the chicken is hot again, it's ready to serve.

Mother Brenner's Lemon Meat Loaf

Meatloaf is a dish that has traditionally been made from ground beef, but you can add or substitute a wide variety of ground meat products. My mother would make meatloaf for us when I was growing up. She would serve it with mashed potatoes and gravy. She would always include a side of fresh vegetables. My mother had a very big influence on why I became a chef. During the process of putting this book together, I came across one of her recipes for meatloaf and decided to include it. I personally have made meatloaf more times than I can remember. What I like about making meatloaf is that it is easy to prepare and you can be creative with the recipe. Doing some research, I have found that most countries around the world have some version of meatloaf. I hope you enjoy the one I have included.

Ingredients:

1(1/2) pounds lean ground beef

1 cup fine dry bread crumbs

1/4 cup lemon juice

1/4 cup finely diced yellow onion

1 egg

1 teaspoon salt

1/2 cup ketchup

1/3 cup brown sugar

1 teaspoon dry mustard

1/4 teaspoon ground allspice

- 1/4 teaspoon ground clove

Procedure:

Mix all the ingredients together.

Pour the mixture into a 9 x 5-inch greased baking pan

Bake at 350 degrees for one hour.

Internal temperature should be at least 155 degrees.

Allow the meatloaf to cool down. Refrigerate for a
   couple of hours.

Heat the pan enough so that the loaf will fall out of the
   pan.

Slice and serve with mashed potatoes, brown gravy,
   and your choice of vegetables.

Carbohydrates

Carbohydrates can be found in many of the foods we eat. Some good examples are rice, grains, sugar, bread, and root vegetables. My advice is to seek the freshest possible ingredients for your daily dose of carbohydrates. Stale food cannot offer what fresh food can.

Pasta

There are many different types of pasta available in supermarkets these days. In most cases, I have worked with dry pasta. Fresh pasta is good, too, and it takes less time to cook. One thing to remember about cooking pasta is it will, at the very least, double its volume in weight once it is cooked. With this in mind, if you need a ¼ portion of pasta, you should start out with half that amount of dry pasta. Another important fact about cooking pasta is that adding salt to the water we cook the pasta in will improve the flavor and texture of the pasta.

Here is a simple ration for adding salt to the water you cook pasta in,

1:1:4 1 pound of pasta

1 tbsp salt

4 quarts/1 gallon of water

I use coarse ground kosher salt. My last piece of advice when cooking pasta is to cook it 'Al Dente' meaning almost done. When the pasta is almost done, it will still have a slight crunch to it. What I do is take it out of the water and cool it off with ice water to stop the cooking process. Cooking pasta like this will take some trial and error. Always read the instructions on the pasta box if you need help with cooking it.

Chicken Scallopini

Most people think of Scallopini as an Italian cuisine, but in fact, its origins date back to French cuisine. The origin of the word 'scallopini' is derived from the French word 'escalope' and refers to a thinly sliced piece of meat. This concept introduced a variety of recipes, and you can find many of them on the internet since most cultures have their own versions of preparing animal proteins. One dish that I served on my menu at Brenner's was Chicken Fried steak, similar to the German and Austrian schnitzel recipes that are made with veal or pork. As well as many Italian and French versions, all based around a thinly sliced and some time-pounded piece of meat. Despite the use of the name 'chicken,' it is made with beef and then topped with white gravy made from chicken stock. The cut of beef I use for this item is a sliced top round of beef. So here is my version of chicken scallopini.

Ingredients

4-5 oz slice of thinly sliced beef and pounded. You can substitute it with a cube steak.

3 tablespoons all-purpose four

1-2 cups breadcrumbs (I ground dried-out French bread)

Canola Oil

Salt

-   Pepper

Procedure

Season your flour with salt and pepper.

Whip your egg with a little salt. The salt breaks down the protein to liquefy the eggs.

Put your beef inside the seasoned flour, then the egg wash, and then the bread crumbs.

After preparation, you have the liberty to freeze the steak and cook it when you're ready.

Fry the breaded steak in canola oil at 350 degrees.

Serve the steak smothered in chicken gravy.

Ingredients for Chicken Gravy

4 oz whole unsalted butter.

4 oz all-purpose flour

1 cup good chicken stock/broth

1/2 cup heavy cream

Salt and pepper to taste

Procedure

Melt the butter in 1 quart-size pan.

Add the flour, and cook for two minutes to a light golden-brown color.

Add the stock; it should be at room temperature.

Add your heavy cream and season it with salt and pepper. Cook for an additional two minutes and serve.

Steaks

During the years I had the restaurant in Eagle, Colorado, steaks and Prime Rib were the most popular items on the dinner menu. Throughout the years, I always offered New York Strip Steaks, Top Sirloin Steaks, Filet of Beef Tenderloin, and Prime Rib.

The steaks were charbroiled on high heat in an open flame. When cooking on a char broiler, you want to have one side at a higher temperature, about 400 degrees, and the other side at about 350 degrees. You start the steak on the hotter side and cook it for two minutes. Next, you turn the steak on that same side at a forty-five-degree angle; anchor it for two more minutes before turning the steak over. Then, turn the steak over and repeat the process. After four minutes, move the steak to the cooler side of the grill. Cook to your desired doneness.

For a medium rare output, I cook it to 120 degrees internal temperature and remove it from the grill. It is best to allow the steak to rest for a couple of minutes before cutting it. The internal temperature is the best way to know the doneness of the steak:

120-125: rare

130-135: medium rare

140-145: medium well

- 150–155: well done.

Remember, the steak continues to cook after it is removed from the grill; this is called 'carry over time,' and that is why I take the steak off the grill at a slightly lower temperature than it will be served at.

The key to a great steak is to use very fresh meat. I used to purchase meat as whole loin pieces and would cut them in quantities I needed each day to ensure freshness. When choosing your steaks at the supermarket, look for the 'use by date.' The meat should show off a bright red color with a nice and firm texture.

Prime Rib

Also known as 'Standing Rib Roast,' this was a traditional meal with our family around the holidays. My approach with a roast such as this is simple: I use a generous amount of salt and pepper. I put onions, carrots, and celery under the roast, which helps at the end of the cooking process because we will use the juices that are left in the pan to make a sauce for the meat.

Then I put the steak in a preheated convection oven at a high temperature, i.e., 375–400 degrees for 30 minutes, and then turn the oven down to 325 degrees. For a medium rare doneness, cook the steak to an internal temperature of 120 degrees. As with cooking, the roast continues to cook after it is out of the oven. Also, allow it to rest before cooking for about 30 minutes.

The weight of the roast has a direct effect on how long it will need to cook:

Medium rare: 20-25 minutes per pound

Medium: 25-30 minutes per pound

- Medium well-done: 30-35 minutes per pound.

Ajus and Gravies

Once your roast has cooked, it will leave you with a pan sauce. Mix some butter and flour with the pan drippings, and drain the mixture in a pot. Cook the flour for a couple of minutes before adding some good beef stock/broth, just enough to create a thick gravy.

For Ajus, just put the pan sauce in your pot and add some beef broth and a little red wine. Simmer for a few minutes and strain before serving.

There is an assortment of main courses and entre items that I could provide, but that is not what this book is all about. I want to provide some ideas and insights on creative culinary from my decade of experience. My goal is to start offering more ideas that will be available for you with the Modern Food Concepts platform that I'm in the process of creating. I will be providing video content that will cover a wide range of material about food and cooking. You are invited to join me on this journey.

253

Deserts

Next, I want to talk about dessert and the after-meal treats, known to the French culture as *mignardise*, translated as 'graceful, delicate, cute, kind,' and 'affectionate.' A graceful way to end a meal. Often, this will be a delicate chocolate served with coffee or some type of liquor at the end of the meal. If you eat at an Asian-style restaurant, think of it as the fortune cookie you get at the end. You may have a favorite restaurant that has mints or some other type of sweet ending that is often free to you, considered as a way for the establishment to say "thanks for coming." With that being said, there are a variety of items you can make at home for your home dining experience. Let's talk about the common desserts we can create before I provide you with some recipes.

1. Cakes

2. Cookies

3. Biscuits

4. Pastries

5. Candies

6. Custards and puddings

7. Deep Fried

8. Frozen

Here are some examples of some of the most popular desserts that are trending today:

9. Carrot Cake

10. Milkshakes

11. S'mores

12. Cheesecake

13. Ice Cream

14. Apple Pie

15. Fudge

16. Brownies

When we talk about desserts, oftentimes, we think of them as just a basic piece of cake, cookie, ice cream, and so on. What I want to cover here is to take the dessert item to a higher level known in the food service industry as Plated Dessert.

There are four components to a plated dessert: main item, sauces, a crunch component, and a garnish. Each of these can provide color, arrangement balance, and texture. Another aspect to consider is how easy it will be for you to eat it.

As a member of the American Culinary Federation over the past twenty-five years, I've had an opportunity to compete in a variety of cooking competitions under their platform. These competitions challenge you to bring out the best version of yourself and help you earn continuing education credits for certification or re-certification.

One of the categories I have competed in several times was the plated dessert category. For this competition, you are required to create six plated desserts. You bring everything you need to the competition and present your items to the judges. In the fall of 2012, I attended Auguste Escoffier School of Culinary Arts and completed their baking and pastry arts program. The requirements included six hours of classes, five days a week. A 32-week program that included six six-week externships.

The book we used there, 'Professional Baking, sixth edition, by Wayne Gisslen,' was an excellent book on baking and pastry, and I highly recommend it to gain an in-depth understanding of the art. Another book I have worked with is *The Professional Pastry Chef* by Bo Friberg, another amazing book on baking and pastry arts. These are very valuable tools if you want to develop skills and knowledge in this area of cooking.

Here are a couple of playful ideas I created for the competition.

Flourless Chocolate Cake, Passion Fruit Mousse,
    Prickly Pear Gelato, Chocolate Basil Sauce and
    Coconut Tuile Cookie

- Apple Tarte Tatin, Rum Rasin Ice Cream, Walnut Crumble, Pomegranate Molasses Reduction, and Specula Cookie.

Yes, these are very complicated ideas. To keep things simple, I will give easy recipes to create a basic plated dessert:

Dessert Component Recipes

Sauces

Whipped Cream (always a nice addition)

1 cup = two cups whipped

1(1/4) oz confectionary sugar or very fine granulated sugar

1/2 Vanilla extract (flavorings optional)

Creme Anglaise

8 oz egg yolk

8 oz sugar

2 cups milk

2 cups heavy cream

- 1 teaspoon vanilla extract

Procedure:

In a bowl, mix eggs and sugar together with the vanilla extract. Whip until the egg thickens. They all take on a lighter yellow color as they thicken.

Use a 1-gallon heavy bottom pot. Put the milk and cream in the pot.

Heat/scald the milk, bringing the cream and milk to a simmering boil.

Temper the eggs, i.e., put some of the hot milk into the eggs.

Lower the heat, and add the tempered eggs to the remaining milk/cream

Keep whipping the sauce as it thickens.

The sauce is done when it reaches a temperature of 180 degrees. Be careful not to get the sauce too hot because the eggs will coagulate.

- Cool the sauce down as soon as it is done.

Chocolate Sauce

1-pound semi-sweet, good quality chocolate. I like 68% coverture semi-sweet chocolate.

- 1-pint heavy cream

Procedure:

Chop up the chocolate, or use chips or coins. Place in a metal bowl large enough to add the heavy cream.

Bring the cream to a boil and pour it over the chocolate.

Let it rest for five minutes. Then, stir till you achieve a smooth consistency.

Cool your sauce down.

After using, refrigerate.

- Warm it up when using it out of the fridge.

Blueberry Sauce

You can substitute other berries or fruits for different flavors. Oftentimes, I will put the cooked mixture in a blender
to have a smoother texture. Another way is to add a little softened gelatin if you want it set up. For instance, you prepare Panna Cotta and custard, and you want jelly on top of it.

1 cup fresh washed blueberries

2oz water

1oz granulated sugar

1/2 oz lemon juice

- 1 small pinch of salt

Procedure:

Combine ingredients in a pot.

Simmer for about 8 minutes.

- Taste for sweetness; if necessary, add a little more sugar or honey, agave syrup, or corn syrup.

Okay, that's it for sauces. If you need more ideas, you can find them on the internet.

Cookies

Most cookies that are used in plated desserts are very thin and crispy. For instance, Tuile cookies can be made plain, or you can create different flavor profiles by adding extracts like almond, vanilla, etc. To shape the cookie, you will need a small offset spatula. If you have never made this type of cookie, I recommend watching a demonstration video on the internet.

Almond Tuiles Cookies

Ingredients:

1/2 stick of unsalted butter

2 large egg whites

1/2 cup finely granulated sugar

2 tsp. water

1 1/2oz all-purpose flour

1/2 tsp cream of tartar

1/4 tsp almond extract

1 pinch of salt

1/2 cup toasted slivered almonds

Procedure:

First, toast your almonds at 350 degrees, about six minutes, until the edges start to turn golden brown.

Melt your butter.

Whip your egg whites with the cream of tartar.

Gradually add the sugar as you whip the egg whites. Whip until the mixture stands up on your finger.

Add the almond extract and salt to your melted butter.

Add the butter and flour to the egg whites, and fold the mixture to a smooth consistency.

Refrigerate your cookie batter. Let it rest until it cools down and stiffens.

Use a sheet pan with parchment paper on it, or a silt pad is better.

Spread one tablespoon of batter, about a couple of inches in length.

Sprinkle toasted almonds on top of the batter.

- Bake in a preheated oven at 375-400 degrees for four to five minutes. You will see the hedges of the cookie will turn golden brown.

Florentine Cookie

Another one of my favorite cookies to use with a plated dessert is a Florentine Cookie. These cookies are usually made with a nut base of almonds or hazelnuts. You have to add dry fruits, such as raisins, and also seeds of pumpkin and sunflower. Just have fun with it, and create it with the complimentary flavors of the dessert you are making. Cook on a sheet pan with parchment paper, or use a silt pad or silicone baking mat.

Ingredients:

1 3/4 cups lightly toasted raw hazelnuts

3 tbsp all-purpose flour

1 orange for the zest

3/4 cups granulated sugar

2 tbsp heavy cream

Tbsp light corn syrup

5 tbsp unsalted butter

1/2 tsp. Vanilla extract

1/4 tsp salt

Procedure:

Place the nuts in a food processor to a finely chopped consistency.

Zest your orange into a finely grated orange peel.

Mix the chopped nuts with the zest and flour in a bowl.

In a saucepan, heat your cream, corn syrup, sugar, vanilla, and butter. Bring it to a simmer and remove it from the stove.

Pour the mixture into the nut mixture, and cool off your cookie batter.

Scoop cookie batter and place small scoops onto your baking sheet. One tablespoon will make a three-inch cookie.

Cakes

Next, I want to share some of my ideas for cakes. The cake will be cut into individual pieces and used with three other components. Another approach is to bake the cake batter in a cupcake pan or some other small frame. I like to create European-style tortes. Thin layers of cake filled with butter cream or mousse fillings. For example, Chocolate Butter Cream Cake, White Sponge Cake, and Carrot Cake. And cheesecakes are my favorites.

There are many types of cakes you can create. In fact, you will come across more ideas on the internet or pick up a copy of *The Cake Bible* by Rose Levy Beranbaum. As a pastry chef at The Harvest Restaurant, located at the Single Tree Golf Course in Edwards, Colorado, one of my signature plated desserts was Flourless Chocolate Cake, Pistachio Ice Cream, Raspberry Sauce and Almond Tuile Cookie.

Flourless Chocolate Cake

This cake is not that hard to make, but you will require a mixer. Here at my home, I use a KitchenAid Mixer and a 5-quarter mixing bowl. One of the prerequisites with this type of cake is to whip the eggs to a very foamy consistency. Another key to this recipe is to use high-quality chocolate cocoa powder. Your eggs need to be warm before you start whipping them. I like to warm up over a water bath to get them to around 80 degrees. The double boiler method is used to melt the chocolate and butter, where you use a metal bowl and place it on top of a pot of boiling water.

Ingredients:

8oz semisweet chocolate, 68% couverture quality

3/4 cup unsalted butter

1 cup granulated sugar

3/4 cup unsweetened Dutch-process cocoa powder

4 whole eggs

- 1 teaspoon vanilla extract

Procedure:

Get your eggs warm.

Put chocolate, butter, and vanilla in a metal bowl and melt to a liquid consistency using the double boiler method.

Mix your sugar and cocoa powder together.

Whip your eggs to a very foamy consistency.

Fold your sugar and cocoa powder into the eggs; fold gently.

Mix your butter and chocolate into a smooth consistency, and fold it into the eggs.

The batter is ready to be cooked.

Use a 10-inch cake pan lined with parchment paper.

Bake at 300 degrees for about 35 minutes.

Your cake will soufflé, i.e., it will rise during the cooking process, and then as it cools, it will drop back down.

Allow the cake to settle to cool it down. You can freeze it and then heat up the outside of the pan. Remove the cake from the pan.

- Cut and serve.

Carrot Cake

My first experience working with Carrot Cake goes back to working at the Westin Hotel, Cascade Village, in Vail, Colorado. This is where I had my first profound experiences in baking. The carrot cake was served in the café restaurant where I did a couple of years of line cooking. Two of the things that I love about carrot cake are its cream cheese icing and its moist but slightly dense structure.

Ingredients:

3 cups shredded carrot; a finer shred works better

1 can of 20 oz crushed pineapple well drained

1 cup granulated sugar

1 cup brown sugar

1 cup canola oil

4 large eggs

1 teaspoon vanilla extract or vanilla paste (paste is better)

2 cups all-purpose

1 teaspoon baking soda

2 teaspoons ground cinnamon

1/4 teaspoon ground nutmeg

1/4 teaspoon ground clove

- 1 cup chopped walnuts (optional)

Procedure:

You can mix this cake by hand in a large metal mixing bowl. Put eggs, sugar, oil, and pineapple. Mix well.

Add shredded carrots, vanilla, and spices. Mix well.

Add the flour and baking soda mix and nuts. Mix until all the flour is absorbed into the batter.

I use a 10-inch round baking pan or a 9 x 13-inch baking dish.

- Bake at 350 degrees. Check after 35 minutes, as it might need to cook a little longer

Frosting:

8 oz cream cheese

1/4 cup soft butter

2 teaspoons vanilla extract

- 3(1/2) cups confectionary sugar

Procedure:

Your cream cheese and butter must be warm but not melting. You can use a microwave. Just do it 10-20 seconds at a time

Mix vanilla and sugar into the cream cheese and butter. Mix until you achieve a smooth consistency.

I usually unfold the cake and cut the top off for a flat surface.

Cut the cake so you have two even layers. Fill the middle with frosting

- Cover the outside of the cake with frosting.

Chocolate Cake / Chocolate Torte

The word *torte* is a German/Austrian word for 'cake', but it is also found to be used in many European cultures. One of the profound differences between an American-style cake and a torte is that the cake's ingredients have less flour and more egg. Usually, the torte will include ground nuts, for example, the Linzertorte, which is loaded with ground hazelnuts. Another example is Sacher torte.

It's not about nuts as much as the overall richness of the cake due to the way they layer the cake. Thin layers of chocolate sponge cake with apricot jam on the bottom layer, along with traditional French, Italian, or Swiss-style buttercream icing.

When I made Sacher torte, I was taught to make a pot of simple syrup and add a little Kirschwasser, or simply Kirsch, a cherry-flavored brandy. When assembling the cake, you brush the simple syrup mixture on the top two layers of the cake before adding the buttercream. With that being said, here is a recipe for the Chocolate Sponge and French Chocolate Buttercream.

Ingredients:

4(1/2) to 5 whole eggs

5 oz fine granulated sugar

4 oz cake or all-purpose flour

1 oz Dutch-processed cocoa powder

1/2 teaspoon baking powder

5 oz high-grade baking shortening or canola oil

-   2 tablespoons water

Procedure:

Whip the eggs. It is best if they are warm, about 80 degrees.

Gradually add the sugar as you whip the eggs.

Mix your flour, cocoa powder, and baking powder together.

Add the shortening or oil to your whipped eggs and fold gently.

Fold your flour into the egg mixture gently.

Use a 9 or 10-inch cake pan, and bake it at 325 degrees for about 20 minutes.

The cake will start to pull away from the pan when it's done. You should be able to insert a pick or paring knife and it should come out clean. Your internal temperature should be around
 205 degrees.

-   Remove the cake from the pan while it is still warm. Flip it over on a pan, then place it on a cutting board or cake wheel. Cut the top to have a flat surface before cutting the cake into three even layers.

French Buttercream

Ingredients:

5 egg yolks

1/3 cup water

1 cup sugar

2 cups soft butter

1/8th teaspoon salt

1 cup melted chocolate

Procedure:

In a pot, cook the sugar and water to the softball stage
at 235 degrees

You would need a mixer to whip the egg yolks to a
thick consistency, known as 'the ribbon stage'.

Add the cooked sugar to the eggs. Be very careful when
doing this; you might run your mixer on low speed
and gradually add the hot syrup to the eggs.

Next, gradually add the soft butter and salt, and then
the warm melted chocolate.

The butter mixture and chocolate should be about the
same temperature.

Buttercream spreads easily when it is warm. If it cools
down, you can return it to the mixing bowl and put
a bowl of hot water under your bowl, or you can use
a torch to heat the bowl.

Assemble your cake as stated in the notes above.

- Cover the cake with chocolate glaze.

Once your glaze is prepared, you need to glaze the cake
while it's still warm. Let the glaze sit at room temperature.
Once it is at 70 degrees, let it sit for 15 more minutes, and
glaze your cake. Pour it on top; using an off-set spatula,
push it toward the top edges of the cake. It will run over and
coat the edges.

It is best to have your cake elevated on a tray so that the excess glaze drips off the bottom edges. You can reuse the excess by scraping from the pan and returning it to your glaze bowl. You can store leftover glaze in the refrigerator and reheat when needed. You can decorate the side of the cake with finely chopped nuts after the glaze starts to set up. Then, refrigerate your cake so that the glaze gets stiff. Once the glaze is set, you can decorate the top.

Vanilla Yellow Cake:

This cake also dates back to my years at the Cascade Village. This recipe will make several cakes, so I recommend cutting the recipe in half or 1/4 for a smaller batch.

Ingredients:

1(1/2) pounds whole eggs

8 oz milk

10 oz liquid shortening or canola oil

1(1/4) pounds fine granulated sugar

1 pound all-purpose flour

1oz vanilla extract

1/2oz baking powder

1 oz at sea level

1/2 oz salt

Procedure:

1. Whip your eggs, gradually adding the sugar.

2. Mix milk-shortening vanilla and salt together.

3. Mix the flour with the baking powder, and fold into the eggs.

4. For a larger cake, use a half-sheet pan with a frame.

5. Bake at 325 degrees for about 20 minutes.

6. Cook to an internal temperature of 205 degrees.

White Cake

Use the same recipe as above, except you only use one whole egg and 1 pound 6 oz egg whites.

French Buttercream

This is a small batch.

Ingredients:

8 oz sugar

2 oz water

3 oz egg yolks

10 oz soft butter

3/4 teaspoon vanilla extract

Procedure:

As with chocolate buttercream, cook your sugar and water to 235 degrees.

Whip egg yolks to the ribbon stage

Slowly add the hot syrup to the eggs

- Slowly add the soft butter and vanilla.

Sticky Date Pudding Cake

I started working with this recipe in 2013. At that time, it was very popular to have this item on the dessert menu in our area.

Ingredients:

9 oz pitted dates, cooked in water and puree

1/4 cup brown sugar

1/4 cup brown butter

6 tablespoon butter

2 whole eggs

1(1/4) cups all-purpose flour

- 3/4 teaspoon baking powder

Procedure:

Cook the dates in a cup of water

Drain the water and puree in a food processor

Whip your eggs to the foam stage. Then, add the brown
  sugar

Mix the flour and baking powder together.

Fold the date puree into the eggs.

Fold the flour into your egg and date mixture.

Bake in a cupcake pan at 325 degrees for about 20
  minutes

As with other cakes, check for doneness at an internal
  temperature of 205 degrees.

Custards

Okay, so that's as far as I'm going with cake ideas. Next, let's talk about stovetop custards and baked custards. One really easy baked custard is a bread pudding. It is easy to create different flavor profiles by using basic white bread. Usually, you will remove the crust, but sometimes I do it with fresh bread, whilst other times, I will cut the bread into cubes and let it dry out for a couple of days.

Using any type of standard baking pan, fill it 3/4 full with cubed bread. Then pour the custard into the pan, just enough to completely cover the bread. What I do is spray the pan with pan spray before lining the pan with parchment paper. Next, add the bread and whatever else you might like. Usually, I will add blueberries and raspberries and then pour the custard into the pan. Next, I put a piece of parchment paper on top and spray the paper with pan spray to keep it from sticking to the custard when done. Then, weigh down the custard by placing the same size pan you're cooking in on top. That way, the top will be nice and flat. This will help if you want to cut it into shapes and arrange them on a plate with other components.

Ingredients:

1 quarter heavy cream

4 whole eggs

1 cup sugar or brown sugar

2 teaspoons ground cinnamon

- 1 teaspoon salt

Procedure:

Just mix the ingredients together, whip it good, and pour over the cubed bread.

Due to the fact that the whole eggs are set at about 165 degrees, I cook the pudding slow and low.

Bake at 275 degrees for about 35 minutes until the custard feels slightly firm. You can check internal temperature of about 160 degrees.

- Allow custard to cool, then refrigerate. Unmold and cut your shapes.

Creme Brûlée

One of my all-time favorites. First, we must recognize the temperature at which eggs are set. Creme Brûlée is made with egg yolks, and they are set at a slightly lower temperature than whole eggs, i.e., 158 degrees. Recook creme brûlée in a water bath to cook the mixer slower and lower than direct heat. You can cook it without a water bath but at a very low temperature. That takes some experience, so I recommend cooking it in the water bath. You will need individual ceramic bowls made for this type of custard. You will also need a propane blow torch to caramelize the sugar after the custard is cooked and cooled.

Ingredients:

12 egg yolks

6 oz sugar

6 cups heavy cream

1/4 oz vanilla extract

3/4 teaspoon salt

- 8 oz sugar for caramelizing on top

Procedure:

Mix your egg yolks and sugar together.

Bring the cream to a boil, and then turn and remove from the heat.

Temper the eggs by adding some of the hot cream to the eggs. After that, pour the egg mixture into the cream and stir the mixture gently. Over-stirring creates bubbles on top. You will see this after you have put the mixture into your dish. If you get bubbles, the best way to eliminate them is to use your torch. Put the flame briefly on the surface of the mixture, and the bubbles will pop.

You put your bowls in a two-inch pan. Fill each container, then pour cold water into the pan just below the rim of the bowls. Carefully cover the top with aluminum foil. Put a couple of holes in the foil; this will allow steam out of the pan so the inside doesn't overheat. Cook at 325 degrees for about 25 minutes. You can cook at a lower temperature for a longer time.

Cook the custard until it settles.

Allow the custard to sit for a while at room temperature, then refrigerate.

To serve, put a thin coating of sugar on the custard and caramelize the sugar with the torch.

- I like to serve the creme brûlée with some fresh whipped cream and some fresh berries.

Pastry Cream

Quite usually, pastry cream is used with a lot of the classic French pastry, such as fruit tarts, tortes, eclairs, cream puffs, and the list goes on. You can mix it with chocolate ganache to make chocolate creme and chocolate pudding. Custards and puddings are different, but sometimes, they can be alike. The difference between the two arises from the thickening method.

Pastry cream is thickened with eggs, while custard with cornstarch. Another important difference is the temperature you cook at to thicken them. This is because eggs coagulate between 150 – 160 degrees whilst you cook pastry cream at a lower temperature. Corn starch needs to be cooked at the boiling point to reach its thickening state. Usually, with a custard recipe, it will use egg yolks without the whole egg.

Ingredients for pastry cream:

2 cups milk

1/4 cup of granulated sugar

1 whole egg

2 egg yolks

1/4 cup cornstarch

2 tablespoons butter

- 1 teaspoon vanilla extract

Procedure:

1. Mix the milk and sugar together in a sauce pot.

2. Mix the sugar and cornstarch together.

3. Bring your milk to a boil before adding the starch–sugar mixture.

4. Once your milk has thickened, remove from the heat.

5. Temper your eggs by adding some of the hot milk to the eggs.

6. Pour the egg mixture into the milk.

7. Cook on low heat, continually stirring.

8. The eggs will help the milk get a little thicker.

9. Add your butter and vanilla and stir to a smooth consistency.

10. Strain and cool the mixture.

Chocolate Mousse

One of my favorite custards is the chocolate mousse. It's not hard to make it, but you do need to be careful with cooking temperature because, once again, eggs are used as a thickening agent. You will need an electric mixer to make this recipe.

Ingredients:

14 oz of chopped 68% curvature quality chocolate

8 large egg yolks

1/2 cup granulated sugar

4 cups of heavy cream

1 tablespoon of vanilla extract

- 1/2 teaspoon of salt

Procedure:

1. Divide the cream in half.

2. Place your egg yolks and sugar into your mixing bowl.

3. Whip eggs and sugar into a thick paste.

4. Heat two cups of the cream, and then mix with your eggs using the tempering method.

5. Add another 1/2 cup of cream to the mixture and cook slowly until the mixture thickens.

6. Pour the warm, thickened cream mixture onto the chocolate vanilla and salt.

7. Fold the mixture together to a smooth consistency.

8. Next, whip the rest of the cream to a stiff peak.

9. The whipped cream and chocolate mixtures need to be about the same temperature. A little on the cool side.

10. Fold the two mixtures to a smooth consistency, and then chill the mousse.

There are many types of ice cream made with egg-based custard. Although there is what is known as 'Philadelphia Style Cream,' and it does not require the use of eggs. Custard-style ice cream is just Creme Anglaise flavored to make the flavor profile according to your desire. Once your base is made, it is placed into an ice cream churning machine that slowly blends the mixture until it begins to freeze. Then you remove it and finish the freezing process in the freezer. So, if you would like to make ice cream, you will need to get a churning machine. I bought one at Walmart.

Lastly, I want to mention some things regarding plated deserts that you can use to garnish your dessert. This part is very simple. It can be something as simple as a fresh herb, such as fresh mint, some fresh berries, chopped nuts, or maybe take it to a more complex level by creating a unique shape with a cookie. Perhaps use chocolate shavings or some type of formed chocolate.

It's all up to you, but have fun with it. I really love chocolate, and it can be a great addition as a garnish on your plate. I would like to recommend a book that can really help you with your ability to work with chocolate, like *The Chocolate Bible* by Silvio Rizzi, Karl Schumacher, and a number of others. It is an in-depth story about chocolate and how to work with it.

Moving forward, let's touch on the idea of Mignardes and petit fours, 'bite-size desserts' usually served at the end of the meal. I have already provided some recipes earlier about some cakes that you can use to turn into bite-size pieces. You can also do this with cookies, chocolate-dipped strawberries, make a chocolate candy like a truffle, or a mint candy.

Conclusion

Dear Reader,

Your meals should bring pleasure and joy to your life, and my goal is to help you create freshly prepared meals that are nutritious and will improve the quality of your life. This is the first book I have ever written, and with that being said, I want to include a list of books that have been very beneficial for me as I have walked the path to becoming a chef. If not all, I hope you try out one of them.

There are so many great books on food and cooking that it can get a bit overwhelming what resource to use. In this day and age, it is often easier to go online to find information, and this has been my motivation to create a website that will provide demonstration videos about this never-ending question of *what I will feed myself today*.

But I must say that I continue to buy and read books. There is no replacement for having a book on your shelf - it should always be there. It's a tactical thing; to touch and feel something that someone else crafted for your enjoyment is irreplaceable.

I would like to thank you for giving me the opportunity to share my story with you, and I truly hope it will help you with your adventures with cooking and the enjoyment of food. I have collected cookbooks and books on food, cooking, and the food service industry for the past four decades. Several hundred books. Here are some that I have used to help me learn and get a better understanding of how to approach the art and science of cooking and baking.

Book Recommendations:

Food in History - Reay Tannahill

On Food and Cooking - Harold McGee

100 Styles of French Cooking - Karl Wurzer

Out of The Stock Pot - William J. Dunn

Food Lover's Companion - Sharon Tyler Herbst

Ratio - Michael Ruhlman

The Flavor Bible - Karen Page and Andrew Dornenburg

Cooking with America's Championship Team - Chef
    Edward G. Leonard

CMC Professional Baking - Wayne Gisslen

The Professional Chef - John Wiley and Sons Inc.

Nutrition Concepts and Controversies - Frances Sizer
    and Eleanor Whitney

The Professional Pastry Chef - Bo Friberg

The Escoffier Cook Book - Auguste Escoffier

World Vegetarian - Madhur Jaffery's
    Art Culinaire Series - Culinaire Inc.

THE ART OF COOKING

The Global Encyclopedia of Wine - Publisher Gordon
    Cheers
    Plating for Gold - Wiley and Sons Inc.

Mastering The Art of French Cooking - Julia Child
    The Bread Bakers Apprentice - Peter Reinhart

Auguste Escoffier Memories of My Life - Van Nortrand
    Reinhold

Gourmet Library - GOURMET Distributing Corporation
    Paul Bocuse's French Cooking